# Mad for Love

# Fernand Crommelynck

# Mad for Love

*(Les Amants puérils)*

A play in three acts

Translated from French by Ben Sonnenberg

GRAND STREET BOOKS

NEW YORK

*Les Amants Puérils* was first produced in Paris on March 14th, 1921, at the Théatre Comédie Montaigne.

Translator's dedication:

*In memory of Frank Hauser (1924-2007).*

The translator gratefully acknowledges the help and encouragement of Richard Howard, *cher maître et ami.*

He is also grateful to Isabelle Mullet and most specially to Tuomas Hiltunen for their help in preparing this text.

© Editions Gallimard, Paris 1967
Translation copyright © 2009 by Ben Sonnenberg

Design by Deborah Thomas.
Illustrations © by Robert Andrew Parker.
Berthe Bady drawing by Henri de Toulouse-Lautrec.

ISBN: 978-1-931824-36-1
Library of Congress: 2009935893

Grand Street Books are published by The Grand Street Foundation, Inc., at 50 Riverside Drive, New York, NY 10024.

Segue Books & Roof Books are published by
The Segue Foundation, Inc., (seguefoundation.com)
at 300 Bowery, New York, NY 10012.

Segue Books are distributed by
Small Press Distribution
1341 Seventh Avenue
Berkeley, CA. 94710-1403
Phone orders: 800-869-7553
www.spdbooks.org

## CHARACTERS

MARIE-HENRIETTE

ZULMA

FIDELINE

QUASIMENT

MADAME MERCENIER

WALTER

BARON CAZOU

THE WOMAN *(ELISABETH, PRINCESS VON GROULINGEN)*

POLICE CHIEF

FEMALE NEIGHBOR

THE MAN

SECOND FEMALE NEIGHBOR

THIRD FEMALE NEIGHBOR

MALE NEIGHBOR

POLICEMEN, TOWNSPEOPLE

*The action takes place on the North Sea coast of Flanders in the early 1920s.*

To the great Berthe Bady

Who before she was Elisabeth, Princess of Groulingen,

Atremble with love's intoxicated despair,

Gave her faith to this image of an epoch without faith.

# ACT ONE

*(The entrance hall of the Villa des Tritons, a resort hotel on the North Sea coast.*

*Through a huge bay window we see only a vast expanse of dazzling cold air. White cloths cover all the furniture, paintings, vitrines, as well as the clock and the carpet. The only objects not covered are the mirrors and the chandelier of Venetian glass, which looks like a huge frost-covered bush.*

*MARIE-HENRIETTE stands at the window, facing the abyss. She doesn't hear the servants come in: ZULMA, flushed with a joy which widens her delicate mouth and enlarges her great animal eyes, and FIDELINE, pale with envy.*

*They speak quickly in low voices. Their speeches overlap.)*

FIDELINE: How can you tell such lies?

ZULMA: I tell you, I was there!

FIDELINE: And you know I saw him at Dumb Mary's burial. And how he swore! And how he spat! And how he cried out for forgiveness! And every time the pallbearers bumped her body in the coffin, he screamed like a woman in labor: "Oh! Don't hurt her!" And how he tore the roots out of her grave with his bare hands, because the roots eat everything. That's what I'm telling *you*! And that was only last week, wasn't it?

ZULMA *(placidly)*: It was.

FIDELINE: And now you tell me he went back to his wife?

ZULMA: Today.

FIDELINE *(scornfully)*: There are more lies on you than there are fleas on a dog.

ZULMA *(laughing, stooping with her hands on her knees)*: Is that so? Well, thank you very much. His wife thought: "He wants to get me pregnant. Then, since we don't live together, he'll go and tell the authorities that the baby isn't his and the law will be on his side." Yes... So she ran around town to try to find a witness. Can you imagine! Everyone followed her, everyone wanted to see, you know what I mean? There were thirty of us at the window, thirty, and each with two eyes!

FIDELINE (*laughing*): What a liar!

(*Enter QUASIMENT, old and deaf, babbling as usual.*)

QUASIMENT: Get up off your asses, you lazy girls! Get a move on! What'd you say?

(*Now all three women are speaking at once.*)

FIDELINE: And where was he then?

QUASIMENT: When I was your age, I walked to the well in my bare feet to break the ice and get water for the entire village. Yes, really... Enough loafing ...

ZULMA: ...In front of the cabin. He called to her. (*She gestures*): "Come here, come here!..."

QUASIMENT: Fideline, take the dust-covers out to the street and give them a good shake, and then Zulma will take them to the laundry room. What'd you say? I'll watch to make sure you do everything right.

ZULMA: But since he was far away, and she wears glasses, and it was windy, she said to herself: "Maybe he isn't calling, maybe he's holding onto his hat." What a joke! But no, he went over and pulled her toward the house by a corner of her apron. "Don't even think about it," she said.

(*Now QUASIMENT is the only one speaking.*)

QUASIMENT: Seems like you didn't get enough time this winter lying in front of the fire, lazy good-for-nothings! All winter long in your stocking feet! What? First we've got to clean the chandelier.

(*Obediently, FIDELINE starts climbing up the stepladder.*)

It's made of Venetian glass, you know. Somebody once told me that Venice is all made of glass: the houses, the churches, the paving stones... (*Making an elaborate curtsy*): They say the water in Venice makes people die for love, and when there's a wind, the whole town sings...

ZULMA (*laughing*): She's crazy!

QUASIMENT (*babbling*): When I was your age, I worked harder than you, you naughty girls! My father was strong and he was smart, but he wasn't brave... A good-for-nothing. So be it: we need folks like that. (*To FIDELINE*): If the ladder wobbles, don't hold on, just let yourself fall.

FIDELINE (*from above, affecting concern*): You can be sure that that's

8

what I'll do, and you'll be the one who breaks her leg, with her hairpins sticking into her skull? *(Viciously)*: Turtle without a shell!

*(Zulma laughs.)*

QUASIMENT *(grimacing)*: What'd she say?

FIDELINE *(yelling)*: "What'd she say?" I said you'd better hold onto the ladder if you're so worried about it!

QUASIMENT *(not having understood)*: Oh, yes, maybe so... I'd throw myself in the canal right away. It's a very valuable chandelier!

*(ZULMA throws herself into an armchair.)*

FIDELINE *(indignant)*: "Maybe so, maybe so!" Madame Maybe So! Isn't she disgusting? Magda, so lovely and only fifteen, Magda's dead—and this, this *thing* will live forever!

QUASIMENT: What'd she say?

FIDELINE: So what if she feeds her vermin with bread that's meant for us. She's not ashamed. *We've* got all our teeth! Ugh! Old people who refuse to die should be rounded up like Turkish dogs and sent off to an island somewhere!

QUASIMENT *(to ZULMA)*: Get up, you lazy girl, get up. You don't belong in that chair.

FIDELINE *(bitterly sarcastic)*: Did you hear that, Zulma? Zulma? Did you hear? You don't belong in a rich person's chair.

*(She goes around the room in a rage, tearing the dustcovers off the chairs, taking the covers down from the windows. ZULMA, scared and amused, follows her, catching the flying cloths.*

*The room, which up to now has been gloomy and dark, becomes a bright and lively place. QUASIMENT starts taking gold patterned boxes out of the cupboards, along with some grotesque blue porcelain figurines.)*

FIDELINE *(complaining loudly)*: Yes, all winter long by the fire in our stocking feet, yes!... Well, now it's over. The rich are coming back, one by one, with their stomachs, their precious bellies, bringing all my agonies with them! Just thinking about it makes me weep. *(To ZULMA)*: Don't you laugh at me!

QUASIMENT: What's going on?

FIDELINE: For three months I'll watch them sitting in those chairs—where you, Zulma, don't belong—sitting and stroking their bellies like little dogs curled up to sleep. God in Heaven, pray for me. *(She looks at ZULMA with condescending pity.)* You're not pretty, are you, Zulma? It isn't your fault. Your mother may have been sleeping that night... Your head is too small and your feet are too big. You're not pretty, but mark my words, the men will say to you: "Not frightened to come to my room, are you, dear?"

QUASIMENT *(smiling, curious)*: What's she saying?

FIDELINE *(straightening up, hands on her hips)*: But you know what I'm going to say one day? I'm going to say, "All right, show me that belly of yours that's so different from my own."

ZULMA *(convulsed with laughter)*: You wouldn't dare!

FIDELINE: "And if you don't have a bellybutton, I'll wait on you hand and foot, you can count on that. I'll make you jams and all kinds of good things. And if *they* don't have bellybuttons, I'll serve your children the way I serve God. You see?" *(Concluding with fury.)* Otherwise, may they choke to death on their cords!

QUASIMENT: What'd she say?

FIDELINE *(shouting in her ear)*: What a mouth on you! "What'd she say? What'd she say?" A parrot talks better than you.

QUASIMENT *(offended)*: Oh! The nerve!... Did you hear that? *(Suddenly, with a ridiculous, feeble anger:)* And I hope a chain of ten thousand lice comes and drags you into the river! And that the Devil will make you swell up in a stove where it's always hot!

ZULMA *(tickled)*: Ha! Ha! That's a good one!

QUASIMENT *(stammering)*: And may you... may you wake up in the night afraid of dying!... *(She whimpers)*: Jesus, Mary and Joseph, the things I have to put up with...

ZULMA: Poor woman!...

FIDELINE *(mocking)*: Poor woman? To make people suffer, she makes little dolls out of candle-wax and sticks pins in them. She's the one who gave you cramps last night.

*(These words make ZULMA uneasy. The girls go on working in silence, while QUASIMENT starts to whine.)*

QUASIMENT: When I was your age, I ate once a day. My father would go out into the fields and joke with the farmers and sing them songs. Sometimes they'd give him a little money... Oh, God! He was such a smart man. Such a good-for-nothing too! *(She dries her eyes on her apron and murmurs:)* What's wrong with my mouth... *(Suddenly:)* Ah! We need some artificial flowers. *(Taken with the word, she repeats comically:)* Ar-ti-fish-al!... What?

*(QUASIMENT grimaces at them and goes out. FIDELINE goes over to ZULMA; they start talking again in whispers.)*

FIDELINE: So it's settled? They're making him leave in spite of all his money?

ZULMA: Seems like it.

FIDELINE *(after a pause)*: In spite of all his money... *(Spits.)* Well, he's infested this place long enough. He's like a little baby nursing for the first time. Each time I do his room, I'm afraid I'll get cholera. Filthy old man!

*(A silence.)*

Maybe he carries all his money with him, sewn up in the lining of his coat. I wonder....

ZULMA *(uneasy)*: Shut up!

FIDELINE *(dreamily)*: Do you think he's made a will? He doesn't have any relations, he doesn't have any friends. *(Excited again:)* The world's rotting, bread's lost its taste! Some people—strong people, young people, people like you and me—work like dogs for that sick old fool. *(Mocking:)* "Mister Cazou, sir, your monocle's falling, your monocle, Mister Cazou!" The miser! One day you'll hear he's dead. He's eaten herds of cattle, including their hides, and flocks of sheep, along with their wool!

ZULMA: Enough!

FIDELINE: They're shutting him up in a home, it seems. *(She snickers:)* Send him to an island! Along with Madame Quasiment! The other day, he told me: "You're a witch, and Quasiment and Zulma, they're witches too. The three of you will always be here, riding your broomsticks!" *(She laughs.)* Ugh!...

QUASIMENT *(returning with an enormous bouquet of silk flowers)*: Ar-ti-fish-al!

*(MADAME MERCENIER, a small, charming woman, comes in after her.*

*Her hair is white, but her face is still young. She has pretty hands and a soft, lilting voice. When she speaks, her words almost seem close to song.)*

MADAME MERCENIER *(harried)*: Zulma, Fideline! (Oh dear, poor Mister Cazou, what a shame!) Fideline, call the police. (Really, such a pity!) Fideline, remind them the season's about to begin. It is, isn't it?... Two guests arrived only yesterday... (How could it have come to this?...) Tell them we've got to evict the Baron this morning, this very morning, tell them. Hurry, please, really this can't go on. Zulma, dear, go to the harbor... (Last night, because of the storm the boats didn't go out. What weather!...) and bring two men back to carry his bags out into the street. Yes, yes... And don't forget to lock the small door... *(Anxious and rushed, she adds:)* Marie-Henriette, darling, don't play in here. Go and play outdoors.

*(The two servants leave immediately, one to the left and one to the right.)*

FIDELINE *(laughing)*: He'll never be cold if he keeps all his money in the lining of his coat.

ZULMA *(straddling her broom)*: "Riding their broomsticks!" Ha! That's a good one!

MADAME *(also laughing)*: Oh, they're young, they don't mean any harm!

QUASIMENT *(babbling)*: They come and go like crazies... Why did they leave? Now it's all up to me...

*(She laboriously starts making a pile of the curtains and dust-covers.)*

MADAME *(to MARIE-HENRIETTE)*: Go out and play, darling, go out and play... Do as I tell you! *(The girl doesn't seem to hear her and MADAME MERCENIER suddenly starts crying, covering her mouth with her handkerchief.)* She doesn't care about me, no pity for me whatever, no affection either... All she cares about is Walter. Go and play! *(She helps QUASIMENT pick up the folded cloths and she sighs.)* Might as well be talking to a dog. At least an animal listens.

QUASIMENT: But *why* have they gone? *(Going out.)* Have you ever seen such lazy girls? *(Her voice can still be heard:)*...asleep at work...

MADAME MERCENIER *(exhausted)*: How alone one is when all's said and done. *(She is about to follow QUASIMENT when the street door opens and WALTER appears. As soon as he sees MADAME MERCENIER, he starts to run away. Calling out to him:)* Wait! Come in, Walter! Come in! *(WALTER comes*

12

*in uncertainly. MARIE-HENRIETTE turns around and watches with bowed head.)* This is the last time, Walter, the last time, you hear? the last time you can come here... I won't stand for it anymore... You're a very nice boy and I'm fond of you... But how can you love such a wicked girl? If you only knew how cold she is!... *(Crying.)* Yes, I'm going to separate you. She'll go back to the convent... You're a nice boy, Walter, but that girl!... *(Going out.)* She can cry herself to death... It's the last time...

*(Exit MADAME MERCENIER.)*

*(Two young people are at a loss.)*

*(A long silence.)*

MARIE-HENRIETTE *(plaintively)*: I waited all day for you... You promised... "I'll be there before the tide comes in." It's not right. You couldn't leave home? You couldn't take the shortcut? You couldn't run?

WALTER *(simply)*: No.

MARIE-HENRIETTE *(uneasy)*: You went out with Julia? Julia came and you went with her to the dunes? Don't deny it: Dagmar saw you. Dagmar saw you last night on the beach—with Julia! You were showing her your teeth, like this... *(Lying.)* You kissed her!

WALTER *(quickly)*: I never kissed her. She asked me to, but I didn't want to.

MARIE-HENRIETTE: Why?

WALTER *(simply)*: I don't know.

MARIE-HENRIETTE: You kissed her!

WALTER: No, what she said was, "Kiss me and I'll kiss you back." But I didn't.

MARIE-HENRIETTE: You did too.

WALTER: So then she said, "Kiss me and I'll give you my necklace." (It's a coral necklace.) I refused.

MARIE-HENRIETTE *(disappointed)*: You could have given the necklace to me!

WALTER: She left and shouted to me through the rain: "Every night you go out on the cliffs with Marie-Henriette! I'm going to tell your mother!"

MARIE-HENRIETTE: What a wicked girl!

WALTER: I ran after her and threw sand in her hair. She just laughed.

MARIE-HENRIETTE *(hanging on Walter's neck, happy, coquettish, child-ish)*: Are you sure you didn't kiss her? Walter, are you sure?

WALTER: I'm positive. *(He strains under her weight as she swings back and forth)*: You won't fall, I can hold you: I'm strong.

MARIE-HENRIETTE: Julia always makes faces. That's her curse.

*(Their faces are almost touching.)*

WALTER, *(softly)*: Kiss me.

MARIE-HENRIETTE: Oh! I'm not afraid to kiss you! *(She leaps off and keeps kissing him lightly, hardly touching his lips. She laughs and starts complaining again:)* I've been in this room since this morning... And you went for a walk with Julia! You don't love me.

*(She turns her back on him, moping. He strokes her curls.)*

WALTER: I love you a lot. You have such big eyes...

MARIE-HENRIETTE *(candidly, flirtatiously)*: I looked at my eyes this morning... They're not so big, but they are very blue... And I do have nice hair...

*(A loud groan comes from behind the door. MARIE-HENRIETTE, scared, stands closer to WALTER. They listen.)*

A VOICE: Ah! One of these days he'll fall down, he'll fall down!

MARIE-HENRIETTE: That must be Baron Cazou.

THE VOICE: His head will crack open like an egg on the last step of the stairs... They've left Cazou all alone! They want him to die. To die!

*(The door opens. Enter CAZOU. He stands at the foot of the stairs, pitiable and awful. He looks like a dressed-up fetus. His weak hands are deformed. His whole body—crushed, suffering, disjointed—stands on two thin feeble legs. Adding to the horror of it all, he wears very expensive clothes, obviously chosen with an absurd fastidiousness.*

*He moves forward and continues complaining in a high thin voice, frequently cut short by gasps... Pressed against each other, MARIE-HENRIETTE and WAL-TER, back up towards the huge, sky-filled bay window.)*

15

CAZOU: Witches!... You'll always be there, flying on your broomsticks!... Ha! You're making of fun of Mister Cazou? "Yes, yes, I'm making fun of him." He was handsome in his day!... *(He makes a face, pretending to be the servants.)* "Excuse us please, we just didn't know!" We'll see about that, won't we?... *(He imitates his own words, tearfully.)* "Zulma, I can't come down the stairs by myself, you know." She was up there, looking over the railing. "Help me, Zulma, darling!...." *(He stops, indignant, straightens up, brandishes his stick. Suddenly forceful.)* She lifted her skirts, yes, her petticoat, too. "Yes, yes, I'm making fun of him!" I'll beat her like a dog!...

MARIE-HENRIETTE: Mama!

CAZOU *(complaining)*: It's hopeless but... He's walked down on his own, making each step of the stairs go *creech*... Oh! Elisabeth! Elis... *(He struggles to take from his pocket a tiny handful of gold coins. Jiggling the coins, he sniggers:)* They're still some of them, there's still quite a lot... Dear little Zulma, cry for me, cry... *(Concluding with muffled fury:)* Mister Cazou will buy himself some tears!

*(The door opens. Re-enter FIDELINE.)*

CAZOU *(suddenly furious)*: Ah! ah!... Evil bitch! Executioner's brat! Where are they, where are my handkerchiefs? I'm asking you! My embroidered handkerchiefs!

FIDELINE *(arrogant, calm)*: You're stupid!

CAZOU *(threatening her with his cane)*: I am... ah, I am... *(A terrible cough breaks from him, shaking, crushing and exhausting him. FIDELINE keeps on laughing.)* I cough and I cough!... Ah! If only I could... cough you up! Cough you out of here!... No strength left... *(A few of the coins fall to the floor. In a broken voice:)* Pick them up, you nasty bitch...

FIDELINE *(mocking but stopping all the same)*: Pick them up yourself..

CAZOU *(sharply)*: No! no! you do it! *(And as she makes for the door, he begs:)* Fideline, *dear* little Fideline!... *(And the instant she opens the door, he shouts:)* They're for you!

FIDELINE *(stopping at once, seriously)*: You are not joking?

CAZOU *(slowly)*: They are for you... *(With a charming smile.)* I sat on the edge of my bed all night, not sleeping a wink... (Pick them up, they're for you.) Outside there was thunder and wind and rain... (That's right, for you!...) No one in the house could have heard me if I'd called for help, isn't that so? And I was thinking, "Fideline's going to come and kill me and rob me of all my gold." *(He cackles:)* Ah! Ah! I saw that in her eyes!... Pick them up, they're for you.

FIDELINE *(hesitating)*: The Baron's teasing...

CAZOU *(fidgeting)*: "Teasing." Oh! No, no, but I can call you nasty bitch, can't I, and thief, if I want to, and greedy...

FIDELINE *(approaching)*: They're for me?

CAZOU *(with a disquieting sweetness)*: Yes, yes, pick them up... Zulma hiked up her skirts this morning... Now it's your turn. Show show me your ass, you whelp of a pimp and a whore...

FIDELINE *(with a crafty smile)*: The Baron's joking...

*(She warily crawls towards the gold on the floor.)*

CAZOU *(grimacing)*: "Joking." Ah! No, no, they're for you... But fair's fair: show me your ass... *(He watches her come forwards with a bitter sort of joy. Suddenly he raises his cane.)*

*(FIDELINE throws herself back. Her teeth are clenched and her face is white.)*

FIDELINE *(hatred spilling out of her as she shouts)*: Oh! You dirty, nasty, rotten old ape! *Fough!*

MARIE-HENRIETTE *(terrified, calling out)*: Mama!

FIDELINE *(beside herself)*: They're going to put you out on the street like someone with the plague! And you'll wait there till they come for you!

MARIE-HENRIETTE: Mama!

FIDELINE: You'll go to the asylum. See if *they* wash out your diapers! They'll leave you in bed, cold and naked, like that baby of Charlotte's that died of cholera!

MARIE-HENRIETTE: Mama! Mama!

FIDELINE *(at the door)*: And they won't even bury you in the ground because you'd poison the grass!... They'll put you in the furnace! You'll burn up there in the furnace!

*(She goes out, slamming the door.)*

MARIE-HENRIETTE *(clinging to WALTER)*: Mama!... Mama!... Mama!

WALTER, *(unnerved)*: You're hurting me!

*(Meanwhile CAZOU, panting, gesticulates towards the door.)*

CAZOU: Thief! Thief!...My embroidered handkerchiefs!...Heartless!...Stupid!...

*(WALTER bends down quickly and picks up the gold coins. Keeping his distance from the old man, he offers them to him.)*

CAZOU *(in a shattered voice)*: You didn't steal them, did you?

MARIE-HENRIETTE *(terrified, clutching WALTER's arm)*: Walter! Come over here!

WALTER *(furious, freeing himself)*: That hurts!...

*(But the old man is helpless. He drags himself away, whimpering, crippled, crying, grimacing like a child.)*

CAZOU: I know you all!... Elisabeth, Elisa, M'sieur Cazou is lonely today... The servant girl said, "They're going to put you out on the street." Elisa?...That isn't true, is it? *(Indignant:)* They don't have the right! I have money, I can pay!... "Like someone with the plague! *(He straightens up again, furious, and addresses the children:)* Where's Madame Mercenier, where is she, so I can tell her! "Wash out your diapers! Wash out your diapers!" *(He spits with disgust:)* Slave! *(Raving.)* People loved him once, Baron Cazou! What! What! Elisabeth, Princess of Groulingen, the Princess loved him when he was alive!... People would talk about it... *(He continues dragging himself towards the door.)* "Like someone with the plague!" Elisabeth, Elisa, where are you now? Princess Groulingen was beautiful! The whole world said she was beautiful!... People would talk about it ... Ah! Poor m'sieur Cazou is alone, alone with his rheumatism!...

*(The door shuts behind him. A pause.)*

WALTER *(fearful)*: Do you think he'll come back?

MARIE-HENRIETTE: I don't know. *(Moving closer to him, tender, plaintive, uncertain.)* Walter, darling Walter, I'm sad, but I'm not in pain... If I were in pain, I'd be crying... Oh, I want to cry!... Pull my hair... No, suffocate me, Walter, smother me in your arms... Maybe you're not strong enough? *(He squeezes her tight.)* Tighter, tighter... You're not strong enough... Harder, Walter, Harder! You won't make me cry.

WALTER *(smiles, embarrassed)*: I can't squeeze you harder, my heart is in the way. You've got such big eyes... *(Suddenly he kisses her on the mouth, then pushes her away, looking cross and mischievous.)* I'm strong enough, but you're cheating. You're making yourself heavy!

MARIE-HENRIETTE *(laughing)*: One night we stayed out late on the dunes, remember? My father beat me that night and the next day and several days after that. He loved me, but he wanted to make me cry. "If you don't cry, you won't ever be good!"

*(She laughs uncertainly again.)*

WALTER: Now we won't be alone in town any more.

MARIE-HENRIETTE: Two foreigners came yesterday.

WALTER: Are they lovers?

MARIE-HENRIETTE: No, they aren't together.

WALTER: Maybe they're pretending.

MARIE-HENRIETTE: No, no... *(Then abruptly:)* Walter, promise me you won't look at the foreign woman.

WALTER *(taken aback)*: Why?

MARIE-HENRIETTE *(quick, staccato)*: I'm begging you!... Promise! No? That's bad... Listen: if Julia asks you, kiss her. Do it, yes. I prefer that. But don't look at the foreign woman!... No, don't kiss Julia. Promise all the same! You don't love me... All right, kiss Julia in secret if that's what you want... Or, no, tell me about it, yes, I prefer knowing... Walter, promise me you'll kiss Julia! As if I could be jealous of Julia. Quite the opposite, I'd be very happy, Walter... Tonight, won't you? You'll kiss tonight, right in front of me... I won't say a thing... Or you'll let her kiss you... She's pretty, Julia, isn't she? She's just as pretty as me when she laughs... She loves you, she told you so... Why are you looking like that? *(She laughs.)* I'm sure Julia told you she loved you last night... Oh, tell me, Walter, I want to know...

WALTER *(embarrassed)*: I won't look at the foreign woman.

MARIE-HENRIETTE *(flirting and still upset)*: How did she tell you? Tell me, it will distract me. I'm sad, oh so sad...

WALTER *(flustered, pushing her away)*: I won't look at the foreign woman... Let go of me!...

MARIE-HENRIETTE *(jumping up and down, having seen through him)*:

You promise? And you won't kiss Julia? You promise that too? She's so ugly, always rubbing her eyes!...

*(Enter FIDELINE, in a rage, pushing a giggling ZULMA before her.)*

FIDELINE: Yes, yes, go on, laugh, laugh and I hope you choke on your laughing! *(She grabs ZULMA by the arm.)* My life wasn't pretty when I was a child... My father came home drunk every night. From my room I heard him get into bed with my mother and beat her to wake her up—and then he took her! *(In a rage:)* I didn't even have a pillow to bury my face in! Then he would beat her some more and push her out of bed, sometimes out of the house, kicking her. My mother... She was stupider than you! *(Shaking ZULMA violently.)* Well! I'd rather go live with her, with them, than stay here serving Cazou! Do you understand what I'm saying?

ZULMA *(smiling dreamily, in a solemn tone)*: At my house, in the country, we never had a fire... We'd open the cowshed door to let in the animals' heat...

*(Suddenly she's weeping into a corner of her apron but otherwise makes no noise.)*

FIDELINE *(bursting out laughing)*: To let in the animals' heat! No, I take it back, there's no one as stupid as you! *(She heads for the stairs.)* The poorest of us can sit down and cry, or lie down and cry, or cry holding their faces in their hands. You were born to cry on your feet, looking up at the sky like an orphan! *(She laughs again, maliciously.)* Come on now. The two of us will bring down the Baron's trunks and throw him out into the street!... Come on, you stupid bitch!

*(She goes upstairs, followed by ZULMA, already in a better mood. We can hear her muttering:)*

ZULMA: Well, thank you!... My mother always said to me, "Irma... (That's my real name. I was Augustine in my first job, with the schoolmistress I was Sophie, here I'm Zulma; but Irma is my real name...). My mother always told me,"Irma, you're as stupid as I don't know what..."

*(The rest of her words go unheard.)*

*(The children listen, holding hands.)*

*(All of a sudden, MARIE-HENRIETTE becomes exuberant. She catches hold of WALTER and, pushing and pulling, twirls him towards the front door.)*

MARIE-HENRIETTE, *(laughing and shouting)*: Out with you! Quickly,

go, you bad boy! Get out! Get out! Fight back if you can! I don't love you! I don't love you anymore!... Get out! Go away!

*(Surprised at first, he fights back without a sound. Finally he pushes the girl away.)*

WALTER *(furious)*: Stop that!...

*(She stops right away and hangs lovingly on his neck.)*

MARIE-HENRIETTE: Darling Walter...

WALTER: Enough!

MARIE-HENRIETTE *(in a doleful, loving voice)*: I'm sad, Walter, really and truly, very sad... *(Then she jumps up.)* Quick, wait for me under the pier! We'll run on the dunes, you'll run after me!...

WALTER: Come on then.

MARIE-HENRIETTE: No, I'll go out the back way... No one will see me... Wait for me under the pier. Go on... *(She laughs.)* I'll play dead and your kisses will bring me back to life...

*(We hear the servants' voices on the stairs.)*

FIDELINE: Go on, go on! No rest, no pity!

MARIE-HENRIETTE:  Quick, quick...

*(She goes out to the street with WALTER.)*

*(ZULMA and FIDELINE maneuver a heavy trunk down the stairs, thumping at every step and banging it against the walls. They talk incessantly over the noise.)*

ZULMA *(walking backwards)*: Stop! Can't you see I'm bleeding... It's too heavy! I hurt myself!...

FIDELINE: Go on! Cry, girl! Bleed, go on! What do I care, no pity! It's your own fault! Go on!

ZULMA: *My* fault? Please stop! I'm going to fall down the stairs and you'll say it's my own fault!

FIDELINE: No stopping! You were going to get some men to help. Go on!

ZULMA: I told you there're no men left in town. The fishermen are all out at sea or back home with their wives... It's too heavy!

FIDELINE *(with savage joy)*: Get on with it! Come on! Stop running off at the mouth!

ZULMA *(at the bottom of the stairs)*: All right! I'm not going another step! *(She sits on the trunk and laughs.)* Look, I'm bleeding… It's too heavy.

FIDELINE: Of course it's heavy: there are pictures and letters in there, memories are in there. *(She laughs maliciously.)* Out in the street with them! Out with the Baron! Come on…

ZULMA: Let me catch my breath…

FIDELINE: Out the door with the lot of them! One is leaving, two are coming! Out! *(Suddenly struck:)* It's really peculiar, don't you think: the houses on the dyke aren't even open yet, no one's in town, yet today one person's leaving and two others arrive—and all on the same day… A man and a woman… Not together either… *(Prodding ZULMA:)* Come on, no stopping!

ZULMA: Wait a minute!

*(MARIE-HENRIETTE, who has stayed with WALTER on the doorstep, comes back into the room.)*

FIDELINE *(lowering her voice)*: Did you get a good look at that woman? I served her dinner in her room and she didn't take off her gloves… Listen, when you think of it, isn't that peculiar?…

*(THE WOMAN appears on the staircase in back of ZULMA and FIDE-LINE, reluctant to step into the light.*

*When she walks past the others, we can see that her hair is too blonde and her lips are too red. MARIE-HENRIETTE and the servants, standing stock still, watch her pass by. She sits far from the bay window, with her back to the light.*

*Long silence.*

*THE WOMAN sees FIDELINE staring at her intently; she bursts out in a fretful rage.)*

THE WOMAN: What's the matter with you? Why are you staring at me? Get out!

*(FIDELINE, turning pale, looks at her angrily.)*

FIDELINE *(after a pause)*: I'm not staring at you!

THE WOMAN *(trembling)*: Go away! Go away!

FIDELINE (*after a long hostile silence, the words like a threat*): I'm going! (*She abruptly goes out, shouting angrily at ZULMA:*) Pull the trunk out by yourself if you can!

THE WOMAN (*in a softer tone*): Tell Madame I wish to see her.

ZULMA (*embarrassed*): I will.

THE WOMAN: Ask her to come right away.

ZULMA: I will. (*Going out, pulling the trunk behind her, calling:*) Help me!... Fideline, help... Fideline!...

(*Exit ZULMA.*)

(*THE WOMAN catches sight of MARIE-HENRIETTE. The young girl looks right at her and, smiling, approaches slowly. She leans against her, captivated, and waits.*)

THE WOMAN: You're a very pretty girl. You're not frightened of me, are you? How old are you? You're Madame Mercenier's little girl, aren't you? What do they call you?

MARIE-HENRIETTE: Marie-Henriette... What do they call you?

THE WOMAN (*amused*): What do they call me?... Elisabeth...

MARIE-HENRIETTE: Elisabeth?

THE WOMAN: How old are you? You're so pretty!... You're still wearing short skirts... How old?...

MARIE-HENRIETTE: I'm fourteen years old.

THE WOMAN (*very moved*): Fourteen!... Fourteen! You're fourteen years old! What bliss!... (*A pause.*) Do you ever cry?

MARIE-HENRIETTE (*simply*): Last year I did. I cried a lot. My father used to beat me...

THE WOMAN: Fourteen!...

MARIE-HENRIETTE: Minus two months...

THE WOMAN: It's true. You're still wearing short skirts! Your eyes are blue... Give me your hand...

MARIE-HENRIETTE (*holding out her hand*): What for?

THE WOMAN (*marveling*): As soft as a kid leather... (*Suddenly sad and weary.)* No, your eyes aren't blue, they're violet… You're very pretty!

MARIE-HENRIETTE *(candidly)*: You're prettier than me…

THE WOMAN *(laughing nervously)*: Child, child! Fourteen! *(More animated:)* Do you still play with dolls?

MARIE-HENRIETTE: Last year I did. I still had the little Japanese doll. She was ugly and I took pity on her. When I was feeling sad, I'd fall asleep with her in my arms. After she started wearing black for my father, I didn't dare look at her any more. *(She smiles.)* I wonder if she can still open her eyes?… *(She sighs and starts to walk away.)* That's all…

THE WOMAN *(tenderly)*: Why are you leaving? Stay here with me.

MARIE-HENRIETTE: Walter's waiting for me.

THE WOMAN: Please stay!… Is Walter your brother?

MARIE-HENRIETTE *(surprised)*: Of course he's not my brother… *(After a slight hesitation:)* He's Walter. *(Smiling, but still looking at THE WOMAN, she moves away and, at the door, laughs gently.)* I'll make him call *me* Elisabeth!…

*(She goes out.)*

THE WOMAN *(following the girl with her eyes)*: Fourteen… fourteen years old!

*(At this moment, the street door opens violently, and CAZOU, bewildered, gripping the door frame, hoists himself into the room.)*

CAZOU. Ah! There, there!… Oh woe, it'll be my death! *(He hoists himself further into the room and calls:)* Fideline! Zulma, have mercy!… *(He whimpers.)* They'll pretend they don't hear me… Fideline! *(ZULMA, looking dazed, appears at the door on the right.)* Ah! Zulma, you dirty little whore! *(But right away he softens and begs:)* Darling little Zulma, help me… I'll give you a gold bracelet, Zulma, genuine gold. Hurry, the thugs are in the street!… Gold, Zulma, gold!…

ZULMA *(frightened, calls)*: Madame! Madame! Come quick!

CAZOU *(in a low voice, quickly)*: Oh! Be still, child, be still. You'll be the death of me!… The whore!

ZULMA: Madame! Come quick!… Madame!…

*(CAZOU tries desperately to reach the doorway near the stairs.)*

CAZOU (*darkly*): That's right!... He'll go to his room by himself!... My poor legs...

(*ZULMA and CAZOU speaking at the same time:*) By himself! By himself! Madame! By himself! Madame! He'll go!...

(*He reaches the foot of the stairs. The door opens. There is FIDELINE, standing with her hands on her hips.*)

(*She laughs roughly.*)

FIDELINE: No one will pass!

CAZOU (*piteous*): Oh! Fideline, why?... Let me go up to my room!... I've been abandoned!... Ask me for something gold, Fideline!

FIDELINE (*triumphantly*): No one will pass! *And she stamps on the floor with rage.* Ah! Don't grind your teeth at me like that. It gives me a pain!

(*CAZOU makes futile gestures.*)

MADAME MERCENIER (*rushing in*): Oh my god! Oh my god! What a scandal!... (*Seeing THE WOMAN, quickly:*) I'm so sorry... It isn't my fault. (*She runs to CAZOU.*) Can't you see what you're doing to us? I beg you, please go! (*She rushes to the front door.*) Don't let him go up, Fideline!... Don't worry, I've called the police!

(*Suddenly, with remarkable energy, CAZOU straightens up.*)

CAZOU (*forcefully*): And I'm telling you, I'll lock myself in my room upstairs!... I'll wait for them there, the thugs! Out of my way! Out of my way!

(*He tries in vain to move FIDELINE. She grabs onto him.*)

MADAME MERCENIER (*running from one to the other*): Don't worry, my girl, don't worry! Zulma, shut the door!... No, don't shut the door, you stupid girl!...

CAZOU (*shaking FIDELINE and with the effort shaking himself*): I'll strangle you! Go on, stick your tongue out all you want. Let go of my cane... Fideline, child, you're making me fall!... Ah, I'll strangle you! Move aside!... He wants to die in his room!... You whore!

(*Enter POLICE CHIEF with his MEN, along with some of the NEIGHBORS. CAZOU out-shouts them all. POLICEMEN seize CAZOU.*)

VOICES: What's going on? I heard shouting... It's the old man... Which one is he? He's that one. What's he done? They're sending him to the asylum... Ah! all right, all right... What's he done? Don't shake him like that!... He's still pretty strong! Where is he? Don't all come in... What about you? And you? Oh, enough, I've got as much right to be here as you! No you don't, I'm a neighbor...

*(The quarreling continues in low voices.)*

MADAME MERCENIER: Quick, officer!...

POLICE CHIEF *(to CAZOU)*: Be reasonable, Baron... You're an educated man...

CAZOU *(losing his temper)*: Don't touch him!... He wants to die in prison! Away with you! Away with you! He'll choke you to death!

*(He struggles with the POLICE CHIEF.)*

A VOICE IN THE CROWD: What a beast he is!

CAZOU: Fideline, give me back my cane, let me knock this one out!... Don't touch me! I'm Baron Cazou, I'm Baron Cazou...

THE WOMAN *(horrified, lets out a great cry)*: That's not possible!

*(Sudden silence.)*

*(The POLICEMEN freeze. Confused, they can barely hold up the breathless old man. Everyone looks at THE WOMAN. She repeats to herself in a very low voice:)*

It just can't be. He's not Baron Cazou!... It's impossible!

*(CAZOU sees her. His whole body shrivels, and his legs bend. He starts swaying slowly from side to side.)*

CAZOU *(grimacing, moaning repeatedly)*: Aiee... aiee... aiee... aiee... aiee... aiee... Elisabeth!... Aiee... aiee... aiee... There she is; there... aiee... aiee... Elisabeth!... Elisa...

POLICE CHIEF *(softly)*: Baron...

MADAME MERCENIER *(insistent)*: Yes!...

CAZOU *(childishly)*: Go away now... It's all over... *(To ELISABETH:)* You're still beautiful, yes, you are... I waited a long time, Elisa, I waited for you every day... I'm not surprised to see you...Sick at heart, yes... *(To the POLICE CHIEF:)* It's all over, you're no longer needed, thank you... I'll leave with the Princess Von Groulingen...

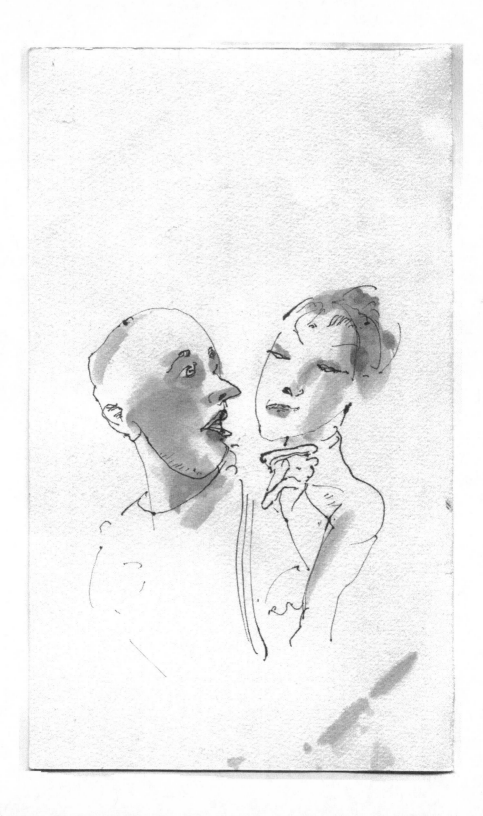

THE WOMAN *(looks at him as if hallucinating. Finally, ashen-faced, she cries out)*: Take him away! Take him away!

CAZOU *(growing faint, moaning)*: Ahh... Yes, yes, I'm sick at heart... The poor man...

*(They take him away.)*

MADAME MERCENIER *(to the POLICE CHIEF)*: Hurry up, I'm telling you, sir. Otherwise he'll die here!

CAZOU *(in a fading voice)*: Just a minute... Give me back my cane... Ahh!.. Elisabeth!... Poor man...

A VOICE IN THE CROWD: Don't hold onto the door!

FIDELINE *(pushing back the crowd)*: Out with you, out with you! All of you, out!

CAZOU *(offstage)*: Elisabeth...

FEMALE NEIGHBOR *(to FIDELINE)*: Give him back his cane.

FIDELINE *(nastily)*: No, I'm keeping it!

NEIGHBOR *(with her fists on her hips)*: You're keeping it? How brave of you!...

FIDELINE: How brave of *you*!

NEIGHBOR: How brave of *you*!

FIDELINE *(threatening)*: Of you!

NEIGHBOR: Of you!

FIDELINE: Anyhow, what are you doing here? Get out! Your milk's boiling over, you cow!

NEIGHBOR: You're the cow!

FIDELINE: No, you're the cow!

NEIGHBOR: No, you are!

*(Enter QUASIMENT.)*

QUASIMENT *(outraged)*: Well now, feel free, why don't you! Come see the kitchen, while you're at it... What's that? You haven't seen the parlor yet? *(She curtsies.)* I do hope you like it... *(She chases them away.)* Get out! Get out! Making themselves at home here... Good-for-nothings... What'd you say?...

*(She pushes them out the door.)*

NEIGHBOR *(to FIDELINE)*: Whore of Babylon!

*(She exits.)*

FIDELINE: That's who *you* are!

NEIGHBOR *(from the street, with a piercing laugh)*: That's who *you* are!

*(Re-enter MADAME MERCENIER. QUASIMENT closes the door to the street.)*

QUASIMENT *(to MADAME MERCENIER)*: I've never seen such nosy people! Have you? They were spying on us... Spying!

*(She goes back to the kitchen.)*

MADAME MERCENIER *(to FIDELINE)*: There's a scandal for you. Quick, make sure you locked the back door.

*(Exit FIDELINE.)*

And you too, go about your business!... Standing there like a scarecrow no matter the weather!

ZULMA *(giggling)*: Like a scarecrow, am I? Thank you very much!

*(Exit ZULMA.)*

MADAME MERCENIER *(to THE WOMAN)*: I'm so sorry... He's been here for four years... I could never get up the courage before... But what could I do by myself? He's a pauper... No family, no friends... Anyhow he'll be better off in a home...

THE WOMAN *(having been staring at MADAME MERCENIER but not hearing a word she said, suddenly asks)*: A man arrived here yesterday? *(MADAME MERCENIER looks disconcerted.)* A man arrived here yesterday? Answer me...

MADAME MERCENIER: Yes, yes... It slipped my mind... He kept you from sleeping...

THE WOMAN: What time did he come?

MADAME MERCENIER: I heard him pacing all night long... He never went to bed...

THE WOMAN *(loosing patience)*: What time?

MADAME MERCENIER *(confused)*: Soon after you… I don't remember exactly…

THE WOMAN *(clearly upset)*: Tell them to bring my trunks down… I'm leaving… I'm leaving this house.

MADAME MERCENIER *(rapidly, distraught)*: Yes, I understand. You were fatigued by your journey. He walked back and forth all night… Those footsteps! I'll speak to him right away… Those footsteps, until morning!…

THE WOMAN: I'm leaving at once! Call me a car! Bring down my trunks. I'm waiting…

MADAME MERCENIER *(whimpering, going out)*: Very well. Oh my! The season's off to a splendid start… Might as well close up now…

THE WOMAN: I'll wait here!

MADAME MERCENIER *(as she exits)*: The neighbors will have a good laugh over this.

*(THE WOMAN is alone. In the ensuing silence she hears slow and steady footsteps. At first the footsteps are overhead and then, one by one, they come down the stairs. She listens, trembling, frightened. She starts briskly toward the door to the street, determined to flee. But just as she reaches the door, the other door opens. THE MAN appears. He is very young and he would be handsome, were it not for a fixed expression of intense suffering. They stare at each other, both out of breath.*

*Long silence.)*

THE WOMAN *(at last, in a weary, doleful, penetrating voice)*: Leave me in peace… Why keep on pursuing me? Do you even know me? I don't want to know you… Once I was at peace, with no desires whatever. I'm tired of all this traveling… Where can I go now?… My only wish is to fall asleep… I don't have the strength to run anymore… *(In a lower tone of voice:)* I don't have the heart…

THE MAN *(slowly)*: Your voice, I'm hearing your voice!… I'm ill too, I'm mad… *(With a calm and terrible resoluteness:)* You'll leave tonight and I'll follow, without a moment's rest. And tomorrow we'll come to another town… Are you leaving tonight?…

THE WOMAN *(in a low voice)*: I don't have the heart.

THE MAN *(with persuasive intensity)*: Then you'll stay? That's good. Say no more, for pity's sake. Your voice devours me. Leave me alone for a moment... Go now; I'll wait for you here... Go quickly: I fear each impulse, each gesture, each cry! *(Adding, with great effort:)* I love you so much! *(As she's about to leave.)* You're not going?

THE WOMAN *(murmuring, in despair)*: I don't have the heart...

*(She exits.)*


CURTAIN

# ACT TWO

*(The same.*

*A bright blue sky with huge white clouds shows through the bay window.*

*THE MAN stands upstage with his back to the light. THE WOMAN, with her back to him, lies on the low arm chair.*

*Long silence.*

*MARIE-HENRIETTE, fresh faced, leaps into the room. She holds a hat covered with flowers.)*

MARIE-HENRIETTE *(laughing)*: I ran up here from the dunes, pretending I was a cripple. It wasn't easy! I can laugh now, but it was hard... Everyone felt sorry for me: "Poor little girl, what a shame, so pretty too..." *(She laughs again, then says:)* The air today is thick as sand! Tonight the sea will shine. *(After crossing the room, she stops.)* Walter's not here yet?

THE MAN *(kindly)*: No.

MARIE-HENRIETTE *(gravely, bowing her head)*: He must have gotten a beating...

THE MAN: His mother beats him?

MARIE-HENRIETTE: Not his mother: the maid! *(Before leaving the room, she adds nastily:)* Or they told him he mustn't see me. He's so obedient... All the same, I plan to die of grief!

*(She gives an odd laugh and goes out.)*

*(Silence.)*

*(THE MAN approaches THE WOMAN's chair. He leans against the back of the chair. As THE WOMAN, weary and smiling, bends her head back, he speaks to her tenderly, slowly.)*

THE MAN: Under the veil, I can see only your eyes and your mouth... Elisabeth! Your lips are too bright, too inviting... Elisabeth. You shut your eyes when you're happy... That little girl looks like you, doesn't she? But your hair is fairer than hers; and your eyes aren't blue: they're violet... Elisabeth! Yes, the child really looks like you. Weren't you just like her when you were fifteen? Each time I look at her hands, hands without rings on them, at her lithe young neck, at her angelic face, I think of you... *(Little by little, she low-*

*35*

ers her head. *He sits down beside her.)* Now you look sad? *(She smiles.)* You like staying indoors, I've noticed; you're sensitive to cold… You tire quickly after a stroll… Please, don't be sad, Elisa! *(Whispering to her gaily, with careful tenderness:)* If you like, I'll take you to a wild place I know, where the dunes stretch for miles. You can't see the land, you can't see the sea: there's nothing but sand, and the sand's almost blue, a mirror of the sky. Elisa! We'll meet under the shadow of the clouds, the passing wind… There our words are forgotten, along with our games. To be without fear, you must love wonderfully. Life is so short, Elisabeth!… We'll be alone, just the two of us, in an ocean of emptiness!… *(He lowers his voice a little.)* We'll go down to the beach, the two of us, leaving our footprints in a dust of shells, so that those who come after us will say, "They walked pressed close together here, here they stopped, here they ran like children!"… *(He looks at her anxiously.)* Yes, you are sad!

THE WOMAN *(sighs and smiles and answers in a low voice)*: I'm happy… You're my friend… *(Suddenly in pain and worried by THE MAN's intense stare:)* Don't look at me like that…

*(She lowers her head. Brief pause.)*

THE MAN: Your eyes have a touch of reddish brown in the blue. I knew you by your eyes, Elisa… *(She gently puts her hand on his arm.)* I still haven't seen your hands without gloves!… *(She rapidly withdraws her hand. Bitterly:)* You know just how to torment me!

THE WOMAN *(fearfully)*: Be careful!

THE MAN *(regaining control of himself, sounding joyful and very young)*: I'm looking at you! The embodiment of tenderness, gentle as a young lover!… *(Coming ever closer and in an ever lower voice:)* Elisabeth! When you walk by in your pale dress, I see you bathing nude in the mist.

THE WOMAN *(frightened)*: You are my friend, be careful!

THE MAN *(vehemently)*: That scent you give off! Fiercer than the taste of bitter almonds!

*(She stands up and looks him full in the face.)*

THE WOMAN: I'm begging you. Be careful!

*(A marked pause, very brief.)*

THE MAN: You know how to torment me! *(She collapses. He rushes towards her:)* Elizabeth! What is it?… Elisa?

THE WOMAN (*regaining control of herself*): There's a storm coming. Sometimes I can't breathe... (*She sits back down. Because of his intense curiosity, she sounds a little flustered.*) Don't you smell the sharpness in the wind?

THE MAN (*observing her, sharply*): No!

(*A pause.*)

THE WOMAN (*not daring to look at him, stammers*): What are you thinking? Don't leave me alone in this silence.

THE MAN (*in anguish*): There's something about you I don't understand.

THE WOMAN (*making an effort to smile*): Take me to the end of the pier. I'm exhausted. The sea air may revive me.

(*But he stands there without moving. He is desolate and bitter, though still full of compassion.*)

THE MAN (*slowly, with a formidable intensity*): For months now I've listened to the waves, rising and falling on the beach. Each night I don't sleep, their sound fills my room...

THE WOMAN (*sorrowfully*): Once again, be careful!

THE MAN: I stand on the balcony for hours. And there, in the dark, all I can see is the light in your window and, very far away, two or three lights on the water. I hear your footsteps. I lean over the railing—.... Too late. Your curtains are already drawn... Everything's dark, and then suddenly there's a shower of stars overhead!... Elisabeth! I can no longer sleep... (*After a pause.*) I go back inside if the wind is too harsh. I lie down on the bed and my torment begins!...

THE WOMAN (*more sorrowfully*): You're going to tear us to pieces!

THE MAN (*suddenly, with fury*): But what made you come here?

THE WOMAN (*with a cry of pain and defiance*): Oh! How unfair! I'm sorry for you! (*They're standing face to face.*) For three months now you've hounded me without mercy—from Salerno, where I could sleep, from Rome, where I was at peace...

THE MAN (*trying to interrupt*): Yes!

THE WOMAN: ... from Geneva, from Vienna, without pity!

THE MAN: Yes!...

THE WOMAN: … from Ostend, where I began to be scared …

THE MAN: Yes, yes!

THE WOMAN: Chasing me, hunting me down!

THE MAN: Exactly!

THE WOMAN *(losing strength)*: For no reason at all you hurt me… I tried to escape from this very hotel…

*(A pause.)*

THE MAN: And now?

*(Another pause.)*

THE WOMAN *(in a muffled voice)*: I don't have the strength… *(He moves towards her in desperation. Horrified, she shouts:)* I hate you!

THE MAN *(stopping dead in his tracks, wildly)*: You're lying!

*(She makes a defiant movement, then shivers and sits back down.)*

THE WOMAN *(with a moan)*: Yes, you're right, I'm lying… *(He looks at her with pity.)* I lie all the time for no reason. Each time I know you see through me and yet I go on lying. I can't help myself… I lie, it's true… I'm so ashamed… *(Bowing her head, she smiles sadly.)* Forgive me…

*(He comes up to her chair, leans against it, then starts to circle it, bending towards her as she twists away. Afraid of being overheard, he keeps looking up towards the doors anxiously. However much she begs him, he can't seem to speak in a low enough voice.*

*FIDELINE comes down from upstairs and stops to listen by the fully open door.)*

THE MAN: Frail as you are, Elisabeth, and however much I love you, I still want to wrap you up in my arms and crush you until you've had our revenge.

THE WOMAN *(as if pursued)*: Lower your voice!

THE MAN: Because of you, I'm powerless, tormented. Look at me: shriveled to a skeleton! Without even so much as a shift in the wind, I'm hot and cold at the same time! And you pretend not to notice—worse than a flirtatious little girl!

THE WOMAN *(stammering)*: Forgive me… forgive me…

THE MAN: No sooner do I leave you in the evening than the thought of you starts to hunt me down ? from behind closed doors. You're there, Elisabeth, but you act with such abandon. I can feel the warmth of your gown on my skin... I know every fold...

*(She seems crushed by his love. Her lips keep moving.)*

THE WOMAN *(in a voice so low he can hardly hear)*: I love you... I love you...

THE MAN: ... and I lock myself in with your image!... Before I'm asleep, if I *can* sleep, I'm dreaming of that gown which for months has dragged me along... I raise your skirt with such tenderness!

THE WOMAN *(a little more loudly)*: I love you, I love you...

THE MAN *(taking her by the wrist)*: I think I see ? I actually do see! ? Elisa, I see those slender legs of yours which so often troubled me, when the folds of your skirt catch between your knees...

THE WOMAN: ... I love you... I love you...

THE MAN *(pulling her towards him slightly)*: ... your swaying hips lulling me as you approach...

THE WOMAN *(looking away)*: ... I love you... I love you...

THE MAN *(ever closer to her)*: ... your breasts, your arms with the scent and smoothness of fur!...

THE WOMAN *(turning towards him in a panic)*: I beg you, no more!

THE MAN: No, no, it's too late, you must know it all, cruel though it may be! *(He seizes her wrists, pushes her against the back of the chair, bends over her with one knee on the arm of the chair and, as she struggles, puts his face close to hers.)* My desire envelops you, clings to you from the tips of your toes to the top of your head! If I fall asleep, you still prowl in my head like a shameless dancer!

THE WOMAN *(moaning)*: Let go of my hands, you're hurting me!

THE MAN: I tear you apart with my nails, I devour your mouth! I try over and over to find parts of you I can't ever reach.

THE WOMAN: You're hurting me!

THE MAN: In my wild imaginings, the servants walk up and down in the hall. In my feverish brain I force them to join our orgy! *(She struggles, but he holds her down.)* I give them your face!

THE WOMAN *(trembling)*: Oh! I'm ashamed! I'm ashamed!

THE MAN: It gets so—is it possible! yes, it's true—I look at Zulma, the slovenly one, with lust! And in the morning, as if it was you waking up from my bad night, I find you faded, tired, old—old and almost ugly! *(Suddenly she's sobbing and not struggling anymore. He takes her face in his hands. He is very unhappy. With great tenderness:)* Desire, like my skeleton, bears the whole weight of my body! of my being!

*(He is about to kiss her on the mouth when they hear a noise from behind the door to the stairs. They stand up, look towards the door for a moment, listen again and move away from each other.)*

*(Attracted by the silence, FIDELINE, pokes her head out and then instinctively pulls back. She waits.)*

*(THE MAN walks over to the door and pulls her into the room.)*

THE MAN *(astonished)*: Eavesdropping, are you? You little sneak… I'll speak to Madame about this…

THE WOMAN *(in a shocked tone of voice)*: Won't you walk me down to the pier?

*(She moves towards the street door. He follows.)*

THE MAN *(furious)*: That's too much! Being spied on! I'll get her fired! Fired!

*(FIDELINE stands still, white-faced and dumbfounded, glaring with her mean little eyes. Then she comes to her senses.)*

FIDELINE *(with brute impudence)*: Oh, no! I don't listen at doors! I don't listen at doors! I've got other things to do. *(But as they have gone out without looking back, she shrugs and gives a vulgar laugh:)* Meddlers! *(Then she runs to the door to the stairway and calls:)* Zulma! Zulma!

*ZULMA (from upstairs)*: Zulma's here…

FIDELINE *(jubilant)*: Wait till you hear this! Hurry! Come down here! Quick!

*(She peeks out the door to the street.)*

ZULMA *(on the stairs)*: I'm hurrying! Where's the fire? I'm coming as fast as I can.

FIDELINE *(signaling to someone outside and shouting)*: Did you see them?

ZULMA *(on the stairs)*: Hurry, hurry? I practically rolled down, that's for sure... As for coming downstairs, I came down...

FIDELINE *(moving back to let in a NEIGHBOR)*: I knew they were together! I said so from the start! *(To ZULMA:)* What are you saying?

ZULMA *(calmly)*: I'm saying, "Be quiet, Zulma, you talk too much." Where's the fire?

FIDELINE *(laughing grossly)*: Under your skirts, my girl, there's a fire under your skirts! *(To the NEIGHBOR:)* She isn't pretty, is she? Her feet are too big and her head is too small—and even so you'll have to put clean sheets on your mattress, Zulma, the Man's going to pay you a visit!

ZULMA *(bursting out laughing)*: She's lying, she's lying!

THE NEIGHBOR *(eyes wide open)*: Is that true?

FIDELINE *(with contempt)*: "I look at Zulma, the slovenly one, with lust"—those were his words exactly—I look like him when I say them!

ZULMA *(bows her head, intimidated, close to tears)*: So that's my fault too? How could I say no if he asks me? *(As THE NEIGHBOR and FIDELINE explode with laughter, sighing:)* Why are you so mean? You're the ones who make me stupid...

*A SECOND NEIGHBOR (rushing in)*: They went out, the two of them?

FIDELINE: Yes, they're together! That's what I thought from the first. *(Other NEIGHBORS enter, each inviting in the next, among them THE QUARRELSOME NEIGHBOR from ACT ONE. She stays close to the door.)* You see, I was coming downstairs, not a mean thought in my head. I was coming downstairs from my room, humming a little song, I recall... I didn't even know they were there, the two of them, how could I? And with no bad thoughts, I was humming... Ask Quasiment if I'm lying. *(ZULMA laughs and shrugs her shoulders disdainfully.)* But I heard these voices quarreling behind the door. What would you have done?

ZULMA and THE NEIGHBORS *(simply)*: Listened.

FIDELINE: Exactly. I stopped on the stairs; but it wasn't me that stopped me: it was my ears. *(She laughs.)* He was making up these fantastic words, saying this and saying that, and all of it, all of it! Just to say that he wanted to sleep with her! As if they could have make a baby just by talking about it!

*(Hilarious laughter.)*

A NEIGHBOR: And what about her?

FIDELINE: She was crying!

*(The laughter stops as QUASIMENT enters, dressed in her Sunday best, with a prayer book wrapped in a handkerchief.)*

QUASIMENT: What's this? Gossip, gossip, gossip!... You're nothing but magpies, that's what you are. Magpies… *(Laughter.)* What's there to gossip about? What? I'm going to have a gossip with our Lord!

ZULMA *(cheerfully)*: He's the only one she can hear!

QUARRELSOME NEIGHBOR: She can hear Fideline humming! *(She shouts in QUASIMENT's ear:)* Fideline was humming on the stairs a while back, wasn't she?

*(Laughter.)*

FIDELINE *(to QUARRELSOME NEIGHBOR furiously)*: What are you doing here, you, yes, you?

*(They stare defiantly at each other.)*

QUASIMENT: What she's saying? *(Chasing QUARRELSOME NEIGH-BOR out:)* Get out of here! Get out! Your job's done here, you dustmops, you! Get out!... *(She turns to the laughing NEIGHBORS.)* Make fun of me all you want! Drivellers, I know what I know! *(To THE NEIGHBOR:)* What did you steal? Are you hiding something underneath your apron? *(She lifts up THE NEIGHBOR's apron.)* Under your skirt? *(She tries to lift up her skirt. Laughter.)* Magpies! What? *(She shoves them all out the door.)*

FIDELINE *(vengefully)*: If she's hidden anything under her skirt, every boy in town will know what it is! *(She gives a malicious little laugh.)*

QUARRELSOME NEIGHBOR *(having somehow escaped QUASIMENT's attention and standing near the door with ZULMA and FIDELINE)*: Look over there at the end of the street: old Cazou with his entourage!

FIDELINE: Old Cazou with his courtiers. He prowls around every morning.

QUARRELSOME NEIGHBOR: What an old wreck!

FIDELINE *(laughing)*: Only the sauce holds the pieces of him together! Time was, people rolled around on the ground underneath his window, fighting for the gold coins he dropped.

QUARRELSOME NEIGHBOR: Gold coins ? Holy Mother of God!

FIDELINE: I couldn't believe it either. I didn't see it myself, but people told me about it. And ever since, the scum-bags hanging around the port follow him wherever he goes. One day one of them will throttle him.

QUARRELSOME NEIGHBOR: He actually knew the woman?

FIDELINE (apprehensively): Yes!...

ZULMA (gaily): On Sunday he grabbed a cookie from a little boy! They fought over it like grown-ups, shouting and making faces. They gave a real performance down there on the pier!

FIDELINE (abruptly): Yes, he's right on time today!... I'm going to ask him a few questions. If he tells me who that woman is, I'll give him back his stick.

QUARRELSOME NEIGHBOR (amused): He's coming. I'm leaving, he scares me; tell me about it later.

CAZOU (outside): Give me back my cane...

FIDELINE: Yes, go. I'll tell you later... Goodbye.

QUARRELSOME NEIGHBOR (as she leaves): He's right outside the door.

(She goes.)

CAZOU (still outside): Give me my cane back, Fideline...

FIDELINE (to ZULMA): Warn me if Madame comes, Zulma; warn me or I'll beat your brains out! (She stands at the doorway and shouts:) Aren't you kids ashamed, tormenting the poor man like that? Come in, M'sieu Cazou... I'll call the police on you, you worms! Come in, come in!...

(She takes his arm to help him over the threshold.)

CAZOU (worried, but smiling nevertheless): You're not joking, Fideline, are you, dear, helping me out like this?

FIDELINE (laughing): Certainly not... (Shouting out the door:) If no one was watching, you'd cut his throat, wouldn't you? (She shuts the door.) But why do you give them money?

CAZOU (plaintively): He's abandoned by everyone, poor Cazou... Give me back my stick, I beg you... He's always so tired, so tired... Maybe his bed is too hard?

*(ZULMA laughs.)*

FIDELINE *(solicitously)*: Look at him: his clothes all covered with sand! What happened? Did you fall down?

*(She wipes the sand from his clothes with little pats of her hand.)*

CAZOU *(laughing childishly)*: Oh, yes, yes, yes, yes, yes... Fell down... The wind on the pier knocked me over... *(He looks surprised.)* The wind is strong today!

FIDELINE *(laughing)*: Not that strong... *(Wiping his clothes off.)* Nothing's broken... There now, wasn't that nice?

CAZOU *(with his childish laugh)*: Ah! yes, yes, very nice... *(Then in a different voice:)* But you'll give me back my stick, won't you? Not some other stick, Fideline, my own...

FIDELINE: Listen to me...

CAZOU *(crying, angry)*: No, no, I want that very stick! I'll buy the beggars drinks so they'll come and beat you! *(Smiling, then fearful.)* I was only joking! *(Suddenly crying out, stupidly:)* Give it back to me... I'll put you in my will, you ungrateful girl!...

FIDELINE *(sharply)*: You can have it back today, right now. Just tell me who that woman is!

CAZOU *(astonished)*: Right now? What woman?

FIDELINE: Elisabeth! *(She and ZULMA, who has been egging her on, exchange glances of intense curiosity.)* Elisabeth! You know?

CAZOU *(struggling hard to understand)*: No, I don't know... You're hurting my head... Oh, misery... He's got nothing left, Baron Cazou, only his money... *(He looks imploringly at FIDELINE.)* I don't know... I've forgotten everything... Haven't I been sick? *(With peculiar gravity:)* Very sick.

FIDELINE *(cold and contemptuous)*: You're acting silly, Baron! *(Suddenly ingratiating:)* Rest a little, why don't you? No, no, no, you mustn't sit down, someone might come... Elisabeth? Elisabeth? E-li-sa, remember? The princess, you said?

CAZOU *(with a laugh)*: Aha! yes, yes, yes, yes, yes, the princess...

*(Pondering:)* They talked about ? ...

FIDELINE *(avidly)*: Really? Where? When?

*(She throws a quick glance at ZULMA, whose face is a mask of amused curiosity.)*

CAZOU: Where? When?... *(He moans:)* I don't know anything any more, nothing...

FIDELINE *(after a very brief pause, bitterly)*: Isn't she still here? The princess, Madame Fersen, Fersen. Fer-sen... Elisabeth?

CAZOU *(stupidly)*: ... nothing, nothing... nothing...

FIDELINE *(sighing)*: He's making me sweat! *(She laughs and says to ZULMA:)* Go and watch out for Madame.

CAZOU *(begging her)*: My stick, Fideline, then I'll go.

*(ZULMA exits without making a sound, very cheerfully, leaving FIDELINE and CAZOU alone.)*

FIDELINE *(very close to CAZOU)*: She' came here with a false name, didn't she?

CAZOU *(laughing again, stupidly)*: ... A false name? Oh, yes, perhaps so!

FIDELINE *(flattering, ambiguous)*: Weren't you once her lover? Her lover, you old tom cat! *(Laughing.)* Your nose gives you away: you were a wild one when you were young, weren't you? And handsome, too. I can tell from your face you were wild in your youth, and you certainly were handsome!

CAZOU: Give me back...

FIDELINE: You were her lover. Weren't you her lover? You can trust me, I won't tell anyone... I'm your friend, you know that... Her lover? No doubt about it, you were still living together four years ago? In fact, I think I once saw you together. Yes or no?

CAZOU: Please, Fideline...

FIDELINE: I promise, but just say yes! *(In a lower voice:)* I'll come and live with you. Just tell me the truth. I'll pamper you... But who is Elisabeth? Elisa?... As if I didn't notice you were after me, you old goat! *(She laughs.)* At your age too!... Never mind, just tell me: was she your mistress?

CAZOU *(laughing)*: At my age... Ha, ha! What age is that? *(He tries to remember, then is very surprised.)* Tell me how old I am, I've forgotten that too… *(Tense with rage, she won't answer. Begging her:)* My stick…

FIDELINE *(brutally)*: I'll burn it in the fireplace!

CAZOU *(very angry)*: Ha! Is that so? Well, we'll see about that. I'll pay them money, I swear I will! Money to gouge your eyes out!…

ZULMA *(rushing in)*: Madame is calling you!

FIDELINE *(to CAZOU, rapidly)*: Be quiet, I was joking! *(To ZULMA:)* I'm coming… *(ZULMA leaves.)* Don't raise you voice!

CAZOU *(crying)*: You have no right to burn my stick.

FIDELINE *(hiding her disappointment)*: Who is that woman? I'm asking you for the last time…

CAZOU *(tormented, holding his head in his hands)*: Oh! I suffer too much!… You're killing me…

FIDELINE *(losing her temper)*: That's right, you old ape! Killing you, am I? Well then, all the better! all the better! all the better! *(She shakes him.)* But no shouting here: go somewhere else to give up the ghost!

ZULMA *(rushing in)*: Fideline, Madame is looking for you!

FIDELINE *(hastening away)*: Throw him out into the street! I'll make my broomstick out of your stick! *(She laughs.)* Throw him out! *(From off-stage:)* A broomstick!…

ZULMA *(shouting)*: Thank you! Thank you very much!… Let him leave the way he came in!

*(She disappears up the stairway, leaving him alone, stammering and scared.)*

CAZOU: What's that? A broomstick, you wicked girl… *(He moves towards the door.)* Dear little Fideline, please don't scold… *(THE WOMAN comes in at this moment and looks at him with horrified surprise.)* I'll come back tomorrow, or the day after, one day or another… Don't beat him… *(He starts to go out.)* Poor Cazou, poor wretched Cazou, abandoned by everyone…

THE WOMAN *(trembling, eyes wide with horror, in a low voice)*: Cazou?… Are you really Baron Cazou?

CAZOU *(looks at her and laughs)*: Aha! yes, yes. Cazou… *(With childish gravity:)* I've got all my papers…

THE WOMAN (*shivering*): You don't recognize me?

(*Enter MARIE-HENRIETTE.*)

(*CAZOU looks at THE WOMAN with a troubled curiosity which memory cannot appease.*)

CAZOU: Yes, yes... they talked about him... they talked about him when he was alive... (*He moans:*) My head... Why are they hurting me?

(*Whimpering, he exits.*)

THE WOMAN (*horrified*): You don't recognize me! You don't recognize me! (*Calling him back:*) Frédéric! Frédéric!

CAZOU (*unable to hear*): He's got nothing left but his shadow... (*He talks to his shadow, snapping his fingers:*) Here, shadow, here. Good dog! Turn left, now right, now turn around, now jump, Sultan. Good dog! Now sit...

(*Exit CAZOU.*)

(*THE WOMAN goes over to the armchair. She sits bolt upright with her back to the light, trembling, lost.*)

(*MARIE-HENRIETTE crosses the room, goes first to the street door and then walks slowly back to THE WOMAN. She stands close to her, very close.*)

(*Long silence.*)

(*Suddenly, THE WOMAN grabs her arm.*)

THE WOMAN (*desperately, in a heart rending voice*): Marie-Henriette! Marie-Henriette! Dear little girl, dear sweet little cheerful child, comfort me, I beg of you, comfort me. Oh comfort me!... I'm weak with grief, Marie-Henriette! There's so much of it in me, so much grief!... (*She lifts up her veil and shows to the child a face alight with sadness.*) Look at me. Don't you feel pity for me?... I'm painted like a doll! Look at me, painted, made up, disguised. Can't you see? Like a doll! I'm old, Marie-Henriette! An old woman!... (*She drops her veil.*) Don't you feel pity for me, child?

(*She weeps.*)

(*Silence.*)

MARIE-HENRIETTE (*timidly and in a whisper, with great tenderness*): My mother's not really old, you know? but her hair's already white (because of a bad dream, they say). Your hair's blond, like mine...

*(Her words are lost on THE WOMAN.)*

THE WOMAN *(quietly, suppressing great sorrow)*: Nobody knows the care I take trying to fool the mirror! I'm afraid of the light, of the wind and the rain that would ruin my makeup!... Pathetic, isn't it? I don't even dare raise my veil anymore, and I wait for the dark before I dare weep! Comfort me... *(Sobs tearing her apart.)* My eyes never used to be this blank, the color has faded away... And without gloves my hands, my poor hands! If you could only see them. Then you'd pity me... My rings no longer fit my fingers any more, each of them, one by one, slips off. I could give them to you if you like...

*(A pause.)*

MARIE-HENRIETTE *(ingenuously)*: I own a ring. This one. The little blue flower brings good luck...

THE WOMAN *(choking)*: I was so beautiful once... All my regrets comes from that, all my grief... I thought being beautiful was enough!... I regret nothing in particular, just the uneventful days, the days... I lived a happy life back then, just walking, without a care in the world. The days... Warm rain in the dust, black streets under the sky, and now and then a street-lamp, and a rose down on the lawn... How it glowed! The shadow of branches on the ground, a dry leaf blowing along... I remember! And little clouds, one after another, floating slowly across the sky, taking my heart with them... *(She weeps.)* Now everything's sadness and sorrow... Why don't you say something? *(In despair, she holds the girl close.)* If only I'd had a child like you, maybe then I wouldn't be sad... She'd keep my youth, my... Her eyes would reflect the beautiful days, her mouth would speak the words I spoke when I was adored! Her flesh would feel the joy I once knew... A little girl, grateful she had my good looks!... *(Suddenly scared.)* And everything's lost! I'll die without God, without children! I'm frightened, Marie-Henriette, comfort me!... *(A pause. Nursing her many regrets.)* There are buildings in the park where I played at fourteen, and the little graveyard is like a city now...

*(WALTER's voice offstage)*: Marie-Henriette!

*(MARIE-HENRIETTE turns her head but doesn't dare leave THE WOMAN, who seems to have heard nothing.)*

THE WOMAN: I'm leaving tomorrow... Good bye, dear child. *(Smiling sadly.)* I'd love to stay in this house, close to you... Oh, I've got to run away again! Run away from what?

*(WALTER's voice)*: Marie-Henriette!

THE WOMAN: Good bye, little friend. You'll still be asleep when I leave tomorrow.

*(WALTER's voice, louder)*: Marie-Henriette!

*(This time THE WOMAN hears. She lifts her head and listens again.)*

MARIE-HENRIETTE *(smiling shyly)*: It's Walter. He's calling me...

THE WOMAN: Oh! go to him, my darling. *(Standing up.)* Go to him, I tell you, go...

*(Exit THE WOMAN, brokenhearted.)*

*(WALTER's voice)*: Marie-Henriette! Marie-Henriette!

*(MARIE-HENRIETTE waits for THE WOMAN to leave, then sighs and rushes to the bay window.)*

MARIE-HENRIETTE *(to WALTER in a tender, light and rather sad voice)*: Is that you? Hello, Walter! I'm so happy! Hello, dear little Walter, hello!

*(WALTER's voice)*: Why didn't you answer?

MARIE-HENRIETTE *(very gaily)*: Were you calling? I guess I didn't hear! Good morning, good morning! I thought you'd never come! I'm so happy! Did you get a beating? Climb up on the bench! *(Behind the bay window, WALTER's face and arms appear.)* Oh! how high the sea is behind you! *(Short silence. They look at each other. He seems sad.)* Did they tell you not to come?

WALTER *(somberly)*: I came all the same!

MARIE-HENRIETTE: You're late... Did they give you a beating?

WALTER *(with a sigh)*: No... I went and sat at the water's edge, just to see...

MARIE-HENRIETTE: To see what? Did they beat you? See what?

WALTER *(embarrassed)*: I don't know... Maybe a mermaid...

MARIE-HENRIETTE *(laughing)*: There's no such thing as mermaids!

WALTER *(harshly)*: I saw one yesterday!

MARIE-HENRIETTE *(taken aback)*: How angry you are!

WALTER *(somber)*: Tease me again and I'll go! *(He sighs. In a low voice:)*

Out there, in front of the dunes. I think it was one. I'm not sure. Like a little shark, white and naked...

MARIE-HENRIETTE (*anxious*): There's no such things as mermaids!

WALTER (*harshly*): I tell you there are: I read about them!

MARIE-HENRIETTE (*close to crying*): Why are you being so mean?

WALTER (*dreamily, lowering his voice*): They're beautiful and they sing. They lure men to a city under the sea...

MARIE-HENRIETTE (*also in a low voice*): Did that one sing to you yesterday?

WALTER: I think so... or was it the wind?

(*Short silence.*)

MARIE-HENRIETTE (*shivering*): Was she swimming?

WALTER: Yes, the waves were higher than me... And the one I saw came closer, closer! (*MARIE-HENRIETTE listens, mesmerized. He takes her by the arm. She lets out a small cry of terror. WALTER, also frightened:*) What's the matter?

(*Bowing her head, she says nothing.*)

(*Enter QUASIMENT from the street.*)

MARIE-HENRIETTE (*reassured, laughs*): There's no such thing as mermaids!

WALTER (*furious*): Liar!

MARIE-HENRIETTE (*caressingly, begging*): Say there're no such thing, Walter dear, you're scaring me!

(*QUASIMENT crosses the room and goes out to the kitchen.*)

WALTER (*hesitant, shy and sweet*): Give me a kiss, and I'll say anything you want...

MARIE-HENRIETTE (*sadly*): No! You're too mean!

(*He looks at her with tenderness.*)

(*Short silence.*)

WALTER (*his eyes full of tears*): Marie-Henriette, why won't you die with me?

*(Short silence.)*

MARIE-HENRIETTE *(in a low voice)*: I don't dare to, not yet...

WALTER *(wild and disconsolate)*: Come die with me, come die with me!

MARIE-HENRIETTE *(sitting on the seat in front of the bay window and complaining lyrically)*: I want to, but just not now... Don't be so impatient, Walter dear... I may be ready soon... Let's live a little longer, a day or two more, even three...

WALTER *(shaking his head)*: How can you go on living? Oh, I want to love just once ? so much I never love again!

MARIE-HENRIETTE: Love what? All mankind, the earth, the stars ? everything we can see?

WALTER: No, not even that is enough!

MARIE-HENRIETTE *(with an enchanting smile)*: I'm sorry, but that's all I have to offer! Don't cry, dear little Walter... *(He turns aside, with a fixed stare. She laughs.)* Your chin's trembling, you're going to cry! *(He wants to leave, but she holds him back.)* Oh! Walter! No! Walter, I love you with all my heart!

WALTER: They'll separate us.

MARIE-HENRIETTE: When I'm old, you won't love me anymore... But I want to live only two or three days more, a week... I'll still be pretty next year... If I was dead, it would rain on my corpse...

WALTER *(stubbornly)*: They'll separate us, I know they will!

MARIE-HENRIETTE *(mournfully)*: Wait a day, Walter, just one day, just one little day... Tomorrow I may have the strength... Sometimes, at night, I lie there in bed, the sheets pulled up to my chin, and with m eyes half-closed I look to see my death in the mirror... Then I cry and right away fall asleep... But I don't dare die, not yet... Next year, I'll be fifteen...

WALTER *(with passion)*: No, no! I can't wait any longer! You've got to die with me, you've got to!

*(Enter QUASIMENT. She starts to tidy up one of the cupboards. Even though she's deaf, as long as she's there, the children whisper. MARIE-HENRIETTE is weeping.)*

I'll go to the harbor tonight at eight. Marie-Henriette, will you come? I'll wait for you...

MARIE-HENRIETTE: No, Walter, I not coming. You must forgive me, but I don't want to die today.

WALTER: And if they separate us? Come with me now and I'll show you the place where I've chosen to die. The water isn't deep there. You can see the grass at the bottom. Marie-Henriette, you won't be scared…

MARIE-HENRIETTE: Why must you upset me like this? No, no, go away… You don't love me that much…

WALTER *(obstinately)*: Yes, I'll wait for you tonight!

MARIE-HENRIETTE: I won't come. You'll have to forgive me, I just won't come!

WALTER *(abruptly)*: All right then, I'll go by myself!…

*(He jumps down from the bench and disappears.)*

MARIE-HENRIETTE *(calling him back)*: Oh! no, Walter, not by yourself! Come back!… Ask Julia if she wants to die with you!… Walter! I'm not coming! Come back! *(She opens the door and slips out. We hear her voice on the street:)* I'm not coming! Wait for me, Walter!…

*(Enter MADAME MERCENIER just as MARIE-HENRIETTE runs away.)*

MADAME MERCENIER *(shouting out the window)*: Marie-Henriette! Mariette! Come back to the house this instant! Oh, what a bad girl! I'm locking the door, I'm selling the house! *(In vain. MARIE-HENRIETTE is far away. Sighing:)* And I'll go away and live by myself… *(Then, half-turning to QUASIMENT:)* I forbade Walter to come here again! See how he obeys to me! I could hear Marie-Henriette calling to him from my bedroom window! Does she have no shame?… If I'd got down here in time, I'd have taken her upstairs and locked her in her room! *(She leans out the window.)* Where are they going? *(She turns again to QUASIMENT.)* The Blessing of the Fleet was at noon. I wanted her to be in the procession; in her angel costume, with her feather wings—everything was ready: instead she preferred to wait for that boy! *(Smiling tenderly.)* She was so pretty last year, standing behind the crèche, barefooted, with her hair hanging down!… *(Bursting into tears.)* If only she was sick, just a little, and I could look after her… *(Then, with effort:)* At the convent, she never complained. She played with those girls in the schoolyard, even though she was getting sick. They couldn't keep them apart. *(She adds with sweet determination, as she walks towards the door:)* One of these days I'll separate them! *(As she goes out, THE WOMAN comes in. To her:)* I'm going to set the table.

THE WOMAN (*stopping her, nervous, distracted*): Wait! Tomorrow morning I'm going to be leaving the country!... First thing in the morning, have them bring down my trunks. I want them taken out through the back door, and tell them to be quiet. I beg you, make them be quiet when in the house!

MADAME MERCENIER (*disconcerted*): Tomorrow morning? Yes... God, what a year we're having! It's going to be a long winter... I doubt there'll be any more guests... Well, there you have it! It's a great loss to suffer by yourself ...

THE WOMAN (*irritated*): Who's talking about that? You won't lose a sou! Swear you won't tell anyone I'm leaving, not anyone, agreed?

MADAME MERCENIER: Yes, yes, tomorrow morning... One servant and the porters, just as you say. (*She's about to say more, but THE WOMAN, who's gone to look out the bay window, turns to her.*)

THE WOMAN (*sharply*): Leave me alone. I'm waiting here for someone! Thank you, that'll be all!

MADAME MERCENIER (*going out*): Just as you say... just as you say...

(*THE MAN enters. He sees ELISABETH waiting for him, standing at the window. With a smile, he goes to her, takes her in his arms and holds her a long time. She gives herself up to his embrace, though seeming anxious and distressed, for all her quiet joy.*)

THE MAN: Here you are, Elisabeth! It's really you! It seems an eternity, an eternity of great hopes and horrors, a lifetime since I last saw you! Nothing has changed: I never left you for a moment!

ELISABETH: I'm happy to find you again.

THE MAN: You're no longer frightened, Elisabeth?

ELISABETH (*moved*): How hard our hearts are beating!

(*The daylight starts to dim.*)

THE MAN (*in a low voice*): Under your veil, your mouth burns like a night-blooming flower.

(*He tries to kiss her on the mouth. She abruptly puts up her hand.*)

ELISABETH (*tenderly*): Tomorrow! Oh! Be patient!... Tomorrow you'll know all the joy there can be. (*In a lower voice:*)... Or all the sorrow...

THE MAN (*in an even lower voice, simply but with a youthful excitement*):
Tomorrow, yes, tomorrow, Elisabeth!... You promised! One more night of
sleep, and then tomorrow. Only one more night!... Since that promise of
yours an hour ago, the world is full of magic! Your image pursued me here ?
in the air and on the water. Your tiny feet ran before me on the beach! Your
toenails flashed!... I recognized your swaying walk amid the foam-flecked
waves! You were playing with the waves like a magician with his leopards!...
No, you were playing with the waves like Circe with her leopards!... (*A sweet
cooing laugh escapes her.*) Are you laughing at me?

ELISABETH (*pressing against him in an outburst of deep tenderness*): Oh,
my dear, no!

THE MAN (*in a still lower voice, very simply*): I saw you. You were
dressed in the wind, behind silken veils, between clouds. Their slow shadows
caressed the sea's surface, under the young poplar leaves which trembled just
the way you tremble in my arms, Elisabeth! It was you, I swear it was you
dancing on the beach, in a transparent gown of swirling sands! A thousand
times I saw you lie down, warm and completely naked in the shadowless
dunes!

ELISABETH (*confused but louder, as if to break the spell*): Dear child,
you're suffocating me!

THE MAN: One more night of sleep! (*And in a dull voice, with violent
concentration:*) If you left me now, my soul would stick to you like flesh to a
burning iron!

ELISABETH (*shuddering, freeing herself*): Watch out!

(*Enter QUASIMENT. ELISABETH takes refuge in the darkest corner of the
room.*)

QUASIMENT (*muttering*): There, there: I can't see except with my
fingers... one day, one day more of life... there...

THE MAN (*surprised*): Am I dreaming?... It's suddenly evening, isn't it?

ELISABETH (*with a short laugh, ironically, dispelling the mystery*): No,
no!... It's just that your words have been blinding us with their light!

(*He rejoins her in the shadows. They speak in murmurs.*)

THE MAN (*pained*): Why are you being so severe again?

ELISABETH (*plaintively*): Forgive me, I'm frightened of us; I'm protecting myself! *(Then immediately surrendering.)* Yes, I'm warm when you hold me... When I was young like Marie-Henriette, I wanted to be in mourning so as to be drowned in pity, oh yes! just like that... And tenderness... like that!... Rock me to sleep... I'm ashamed to be so happy... Spare me!

*(Kneeling on the chair, he takes her hands. She leans towards him a little in the deepening twilight.)*

THE MAN *(happily)*: Elisabeth! I've spared you for weeks so that tomorrow I could have you all to myself!

ELISABETH *(taking his head between her hands, with infinite tenderness)*: Child! Dear child...

THE MAN: I've caressed the air between us, molded it to make a space where I can look for your shape. I've done this so often so that today, because of my gestures of adoration, you could come into being like a statue of bronze, the mold finally broken ? *(She laughs again, a sweet, tender laugh.)* Why do you always laugh at me?

ELISABETH *(raising her voice)*: I'm laughing at the things you say! *(Suddenly sad.)* I'm nothing to you but a dream, like all the other dreams you play with!... *(Then whispering:)* Yes, I love you like that!...

*(She kisses him on the mouth, then rises and moves away. He keeps hold of her hand, pressing it against his forehead, leaning towards her a moment in an attitude of overwhelming joy.*

*A long silence follows, a silence filled first with emotion, then with surprise. He raises his head, looks at ELISABETH, then stands up and tries to embrace her. She pushes him away.)*

THE MAN *(softly, almost painfully)*: Elisabeth! What's the matter?

ELISABETH *(facing him and in an almost too clear voice, with a factitious joy)*: Oh, nothing's the matter, nothing at all, nothing!...

THE MAN *(not fooled, pulling her towards him)*: What makes you so sad, you who give so much joy?

ELISABETH *(with renewed abandon)*: Don't speak!... I'm afraid of making you suffer, inconceivably and for ever! I beg for your forgiveness in advance... *(Then suddenly, feverishly:)* Swear you won't hold me back tomorrow the way you did today.

THE MAN *(full of hope)*: Tomorrow!

ELISABETH *(with a nervous laugh)*: Oh, I was so frightened! Every time you looked at me, my life leaked away as if through an invisible wound… My blood froze… I was too scared, too weak back then. I longed to be carried up to my bedroom by you…

THE MAN: Tomorrow!

ELISABETH *(pressed against him, no longer laughing but dreaming, and filled with drunken despair)*: Too scared! In the blue water, there are green streams… I could see them from my window… And your desire filled me with its continuous caressing strength… *(In a lower voice:)* Is it quite dark?… *(In a feverish whisper:)* A moment ago my lips were pressed against your heart, your mouth was so hot!

THE MAN: Have you no pity!

ELISABETH *(moaning)*: Oh! my love, you mean well, but you hurt me! *(She moves farther away. With a melancholy smile:)* I beg your forgiveness, I'll often be sad… But I love you, I really do… *(She hesitates. Stammering:)*… and I'm no longer young… *(Yet she clings to him fiercely, growing more and more feverish. Speaking fast, between bursts of laughter and tears. The pair of them are like shadows on the screen of the bay window.)* No! No, it's nothing whatever! Look at me! You know how much I love you! Maybe a miracle… No future, no past: just one day, a day without hours, one everlasting day!… My love, are you looking at me? I can't see your eyes. I feel them on my skin like warm rain!… Even so, I'm sad. You can't tell the whole truth to someone you love … Closer! In my room, at night, a scent of amber… as though you were there… my heart took flight!… *(Is she crying? After a very short pause:)* No, no, wait, be still! If you speak, I'll break down in tears!

*(QUASIMENT stands up, slams the cupboard door shut, lifts the bunch of silk flowers from the table, shakes them and cradles them in her arms.)*

QUASIMENT *(grotesquely)*: Artificial! Ar-ti-fi-cial flowers?

*(She goes out.)*

*(ELISABETH and THE MAN, surprised, move apart from each other. A short pause, then he lets out a loud, joyous laugh.)*

THE MAN: Oh! That pathetic Quasiment! We forgot all about her!

*(Silence.)*

*(He walks in front of the distant bay window. We can barely make him out. Lowering his voice a little:)* Why don't you answer? *(He laughs.)* She was hiding

like an owl in our landscape. Are you frightened?... Don't be: she's deaf. And even if she saw us, she's too old to understand! *(ELISABETH utters a cry of pain. He goes to her.)* What's the matter? Stand here close to me... You're shaking all over! Are you ill?

ELISABETH *(in a dull voice)*: Farewell!... Bid me farewell!

THE MAN: Why are you running away?

ELISABETH *(delirious)*: I lied! Each word I spoke was a lie! No, don't hold me back. I lied, I was out of my mind! Anyone but you! Some are cruel and cowardly, yes!...

THE MAN *(holding her)*: Come to me, come here!

ELISABETH, *(rushing her words in a trembling, broken voice)*: ... Someone who'd despise me, maybe even a little too much... Yes, that kind of man, but not you! And I've been unfaithful: I swear to you by all I hold dear! Go now, I beg of you. Our lives will never match like two eyes in one face!

THE MAN *(confident)*: I'm holding you with all my might!

ELISABETH *(resisting)*: Oh no, let go of me, no! Each hour of abandon will only tear us farther apart. Is it my fault? *(She lowers her voice.)* You came to me. And now, in the shadow you cast, I see nothing but a vast desert.

THE MAN: Till tomorrow!

ELISABETH *(overflowing with bitter hope)*: Tomorrow? Oh, yes, tomorrow I'll leave! I'll go, I'll go... departures, road signs, the names of towns, signs, signs... what's the use, nowhere to stop, nowhere! Nowhere on earth can I find my own narrow grave! And yet I'll go on...

THE MAN *(still tense, still joyful)*: Elisabeth! You can no longer leave me! *I* will be your grave. Only promise me that tomorrow you'll be as beautiful as when you die.

ELISABETH *(in a white, frozen voice)*: I'm cold... can't you feel how cold I am? Maybe the night is inside me now.

THE MAN: Do you want more light?

ELISABETH *(a cry of terror)*: No!... You're abandoning me in the dark... Hold me close. I feel warm in your arms. It's true, I've always been scared of the dark... *(Trying to laugh:)* And I've been crying so much, I must be ugly... No, no.

THE MAN: Tomorrow I'll clasp your image so tight, I'll be the clothes of your naked youth. You'll be dead and yet you won't be dead. And when I go to the graveyard, I'll go on a morning in May. I'll be as merry as a miller, with my head held high and my collar open, and my hands in my trouser pockets. I'll be whistling a merry tune and people will say how heartless he is! *(He laughs, then with sudden compassion:)* Oh, you really *are* shivering.

ELISABETH: It's nothing... I'll go fetch a shawl...

THE MAN: Yes, yes, go... *(He takes her to the door to the stairs.)* I'll clamber up an apple tree and I'll break off a branch and I'll swing it through the air and then I'll give it to you... And I'll say: I am her scarf and her rings, I am her sandals and her smile, I am her dreams and her sleep! Yes, go... Ungrateful woman, you're eager to go!

ELISABETH *(once more trying to laugh)*: Oh! no, but watch out, they might catch us... Don't kiss me! I'll be back...

THE MAN *(very softly, very simply)*: Yes, you'll be back. And so farewell! In an hour?

ELISABETH *(going out)*: Yes...

THE MAN *(in a muted voice)*: I'm a little crazy!... *(Pause.)* I'll be waiting for you... Farewell, madame. *(Pause.)* Tomorrow!... *(Pause.)* Farewell...

*(A silence.)*

*( Suddenly light fills the room. And there is FIDELINE.)*

*(In front of the window, THE MAN looks out to sea.)*

FIDELINE *(a cry of terror)*: Oh my god! *(After a pause, she laughs in a sly, provocative way, checking every corner of the room.)* I didn't hear anything, I thought I was alone... Dinner is served, M'sieur. *(He turns around, holding his hand up against the light, and stares at her in confusion. She laughs her arch and impudent laugh.)* The light blinds you... Should I turn it off? I can wait... *(He doesn't answer. Her laughter stops.)* Today we're having shrimp bisque, oysters, roast lamb... *(He passes in front of her. She doesn't lower her eyes. With an ambiguous laugh:)*... cold chicken, salad with a ginger dressing...

THE MAN *(indifferently)*: Thank you...

*(Exit THE MAN. She watches him go and gives a dry, mocking laugh.)*

FIDELINE *(between clenched teeth)*: I made up the menu myself!

*(She looks up the dark stairs, listens intently, shrugs her shoulders and walks towards the window and cries with impatience:)* Child! Child! *(And suddenly, leaning out the window, she shouts.)* Marie-Henriette! Marie-Henriette! Now what? *(Pause.)* Hurry! *(Pause.)* The tables are set. *(Pause.)* Your mother's waiting! Where are you? *(She comes back inside. No sooner has she closed the window than MARIE-HENRIETTE re-appears. She walks by quickly, her head down. FIDELINE looks at her inquisitively. As she is about to exit, FIDELINE calls out:)* Marie-Henriette! *(And as the girl pays no attention, she shouts:)* I'm going to Walter's mother's house! *(MARIE-HENRIETTE doesn't stop. FIDELINE goes to the door to the street.)* I'm leaving right now!

*(MARIE-HENRIETTE turns back abruptly, with a pained expression.)*

MARIE-HENRIETTE: Oh no! Why!... Why, why...

FIDELINE *(taken aback)*: Answer me when I'm talking to you!

MARIE-HENRIETTE *(hardly audibly)*: ...why?...

FIDELINE *(in a softer tone)*: From the kitchen just now, I saw you and that woman together. What was she telling you?

MARIE-HENRIETTE *(suddenly hostile)*: Nothing! Nothing! Leave me alone!... I don't want to tell you, you nasty little creature!... I'm not telling you a thing!

FIDELINE *(moving towards the door)*: I'm leaving!

MARIE-HENRIETTE *(very quickly, with fury)*: Go on! Go! I couldn't care less!... Go or don't go, you nasty pest, I'm not telling you a thing! I don't care! *(And as FIDELINE is about to go out, she jumps in front of the door instead. Resolutely:)* You can't go!

FIDELINE *(very calmly)*: Now, I'm not going to fight with you, Marie-Henriette, but you can't stand there forever...

MARIE-HENRIETTE *(with certainty)*: Oh, yes, I can! You won't get out!

FIDELINE *(turning her back)*: All right, we'll soon see...

*(She starts towards the kitchen. MARIE-HENRIETTE brings her to a stop.)*

MARIE-HENRIETTE *(savagely)*: She asked me how old I was...

*(She lowers her head for a moment.)*

FIDELINE: And what did she say then?... She couldn't have been crying for so long over that? *(After a pause.)* I'm going, I'm going...

MARIE-HENRIETTE *(in agony)*: She said she was leaving tomorrow.

FIDELINE: Leaving tomorrow? Yes... And what else? *(Pauses.)* If I go to Walter's mother, they'll separate you...

MARIE-HENRIETTE *(with tears in her eyes)*: ...That she was old... that's all I remember, that she was old. That's all...

FIDELINE *(surprised at first)*: That she's old? *(A pause. She looks acutely at MARIE-HENRIETTE. And suddenly she understands. Her body stiffens and a diabolical joy sets her face alight. Radiantly:)* Yes! Yes! Yes! Yes! And that's why she's always sitting down... Of course! And always with her back to the light! She's as old as your mother, isn't she? As old as Quasiment? Yes! And in the evening, she likes the lights turned down. So that's how it is! And Cazou? Cazou!... So that's how it is!... *(She laughs.)* Now I'm not going, Marie-Henriette... Anyhow I was just joking... Come on now, stop crying. I was joking!... Quick now, the table's all set...

MARIE-HENRIETTE *(going out, murmuring)*: Why... why?... The nasty creature!...

*(As soon as she goes, FIDELINE runs to the street door, opens it, looks out and calls in a muffled voice:)*

FIDELINE: Julia!... Julia!... Charlotte! *(She comes back in, goes to the door to the stairs and calls again.)* Zulma! Come down here, Zulma! Come down!... *(She goes back to the door to the street. Apparently somebody's coming. She calls with impatient joy:)* Everyone, come quickly!

CURTAIN

*(The same.*

*The bay window is wide open. From far down the dike, over an abyss of darkness, like tiny moons float little spheres of light. This light show invades the room, like a reverberant snowfall. It decorates the sides of furniture, other objects as well, carving out large blocks of shadow.*

*The crystal chandelier, immersed in bluish shadow in the center of a leaden ceiling, is like a big bush of stars.*

*MARIE-HENRIETTE, alone by the window, sits with her elbows on her knees, her chin resting in her hands.*

*Two young voices are heard from outside.)*

THE VOICES: Up to the signal lantern!... Hey, I'm going down to the dunes! The edge of the sea's on fire!

MARIE-HENRIETTE *(dreaming, in low voice)*: Walter?... My darling Wal...

THE VOICES *(among them a clear laugh)*: Oh! Oh! I've got nothing on under my dress! I've let my hair down! Let's go into the surf!

*(THE VOICES grow faint.)*

*(A silence.)*

MARIE-HENRIETTE *(calling softly, in a voice that seems suspended)*: Walter? Come to me, oh yes, come...

THE DISTANT VOICES: Oh-ho!... Oh-ho!...

MARIE-HENRIETTE: I see you: you're standing still. Why so long? Walter, how black your shadow is... and long, so very long! It reaches up to the very last house... It fastens you to the gold light in the window... Yes, jump into the surf if you want, it'll bring you back to shore!... *(She just barely laughs before saying:)* Are you sulking?... As for myself, I'm waiting for you. Don't come and I'll think you're with Julia... *(Silence. She seems to be listening. Cajolingly:)* Of course I'm fond of you, darling Wal, as sweet a boy as ever there was... Oh, how I love you, I love you!... *(She sighs and rests her cheek on her hands. She holds her hands close together and then starts kissing them softly.)* I love you so much! You're in my prayers at bedtime and at night you're in my dreams. What can I do?... And in my sleep even when I'm not dreaming... Walter? And always, always... *(Another silence. She starts singing in a low voice to herself.)* No, no, I can't walk on water... *(Then in a natural tone with all the modulations of a lively conversation:)* But maybe I could... Sometimes the sea looks like cold marble to me: I could set out then if I went barefoot. Otherwise the sea would get into my shoes and pull me down under the waves!... *(She laughs.)* Run, run! You'll catch me! Ah! you're falling down in the sand! Here we are: you don't have enough breath to kiss me even once!

FIDELINE'S VOICE *(from the next room)*: There now, my girl, I'm leaving!

VOICES OUTSIDE *(calling from a distance)*: To the sea! To the sea! In the dunes!

*(Enter ZULMA and FIDELINE.)*

*(ZULMA carries a lamp with a gigantic lampshade. FIDELINE, wearing her best clothes, even a hat, pulls on her gloves.)*

FIDELINE *(giddy, insolent, talkative)*: I'm quitting, that's all there is to it! Nobody fires me, I quit... Anyhow, Madame's so soft, you could cut her in half with a ribbon!

ZULMA *(chuckling)*: Oh! yes indeed, with a ribbon!

FIDELINE: I prefer to quit: I'm quitting, no more and no less. Besides, Baron Cazou is waiting for me, poor dear innocent Cazou...

*(She laughs.)*

ZULMA *(amused)*: Will you sleep with him tonight?

FIDELINE: If he puts me in his will! Either tonight or tomorrow...

ZULMA *(worried)*: Hush!...

FIDELINE: Anyhow, I'll know how to cuddle him! "Oh, nice Baron! *Naughty* Baron!" *(Grimacing with disgust.)* Faugh! *(Then sighing.)* Be patient, Fideline, money doesn't grow on trees!

VOICES *(outside)*: The lights of the boats!... Oh! oh!... There, behind the pier!... Oh!...

ZULMA *(dreaming, ingenuous)*: Trees, yes... In the garden of my first job, there was only one tree, a peach tree with just one peach... In the morn-

62

ing, I'd watch it ripen… (My apron was still longer than my skirt, I may say…) And then one Sunday, I ate it… the peach… and they fired me: they'd been watching it, too.

*(Short silence.)*

DISTANT VOICES: Oh! oh! Here!… The tide's coming in!

FIDELINE *(laughing)*: Oh! Put the lamp down; there you go, casting light on your stupidity, like a lovelorn girl waiting up for her man after midnight…

ZULMA *(taken aback)*: You're mean!

FIDELINE *(bitingly)*: And you're nice, that's for sure! It's nice how your meaty legs open as wide as the arms of Our Lord! Ha! Ha!… Here's where I leave you, you nice girl… Soon the mice and the moths will eat up the house! Let the wind blow it away! I'm leaving… *(She goes to the door.)* Cazou's waiting for me in his wheelchair… *(She turns around abruptly.)* You don't believe he begged me? I'm telling you it's true! Not an hour ago, he was here on his knees: all shriveled up!… Good night…

ZULMA: Good night…

*(She moves towards the kitchen. But FIDELINE runs after her and grabs her.)*

FIDELINE: And I'm leaving you with the stranger, to each her own! Ha! Ha!… *(She lowers her voice and says, very agitated:)* You'll see some great things, you slave, you, if you've got eyes in your head… Tonight, tonight!… The princess and Cazou!… Ha! Ha! What a puppet show! *(In a still lower voice:)* She's old, believe me; a stuffed carcass, painted plaster, varnished over and so dried out, you could put her with the kitchen herbs! Ha! Ha! She can eat all the fatty foods she wants, she won't put on an ounce! *(She shoves ZULMA away and goes towards the door.)* Good night… Remember how she looked me up and down?… I know her now and I'm telling you, it's a miracle she can walk!

*(She opens the door.)*

ZULMA *(already cheerful)*: Good night…

*(Going out, FIDELINE catches sight of MARIE-HENRIETTE.)*

FIDELINE *(with redoubled energy)*: Oh! Is that you, M'selle? Calm down, he won't be coming. He's being punished, put in the cellar where the rats and beetles are! Or else he's with Julia out on the dunes, teaching her how to count stars without having to twist her neck. Ha! Ha! I'm leaving, I'm leaving… *(She turns her back on MARIE-HENRIETTE who goes stiff with fear.)* Love him anyhow, and quickly. I'm telling you, it won't last… You won't always be sweet and pretty and loved… Good night… *(She goes out again and again comes back.)* But who knows, maybe he *will* come. One day Christine's lover came back and it was a disaster. He'd gone overseas to find gold… For five years she waited for him, alone in her room with his picture! She'd wake up at night and gaze at it: until she knew him by heart, so to speak. *(Abruptly, to ZULMA:)* Don't tell me no, that's how it was!

ZULMA *(solemnly)*: She had nothing else in her life ? just him and her grief?

FIDELINE *(continuing)*: And then one fine day, without warning, there he was at her door!… She didn't exactly fall down on the spot and die of happiness… He'd been hungry and cold and sick with all different kinds of disease. Sometimes, thinking about her, he'd tear his hair out and weep! For her! For Christine! In short, he wasn't the man she remembered… And yet, there he was!… She said, "Where's the man I've been waiting for? Where is he now? You've changed quite a bit…"

MARIE-HENRIETTE *(tensely)*: Be quiet!

FIDELINE *(laughing)*: "I suffered so much," he told her. "Poor man," she replied. "Did you *have* to? Suffering ruins your looks."

MARIE-HENRIETTE *(in a burst of rage)*: Liar! Liar! Go away!

FIDELINE: "… ruins your looks. Is it my fault?" And she didn't want him any more.

MARIE-HENRIETTE *(white with anger)*: Liar! Go away!

FIDELINE *(going towards the door, exhilarated)*: Ha! Ha! It's always the same old story! What else can you expect from love? Goodbye all!

*(She opens the door.)*

ZULMA *(smiling fondly)*: You're leaving and I'm sad, in spite of you being so nasty to me. Isn't that funny?…

FIDELINE *(on the doorstep, with a dry, fierce laugh)*: Thank you, my girl! And when I inherit his money, I'll save you his false teeth. But don't count on it being soon. In spite of my best efforts, he'll hang on for as long as he can!… You're a good girl, thank you… *(She goes, but half out the door, she leans back in towards ZULMA.)* And may you have twelve sons: three of them gimpy and one with bowlegs, three of them with hunch backs and one who's a gnome, and three of them without hair and one with a pointy head.

*(She slams the door shut.)*

*(Stunned at first, ZULMA giggles.)*

ZULMA *(as she disappears under the stairs, with a laugh)*: Isn't she too much!

*(MARIE-HENRIETTE is alone. But then the door re-opens slightly.)*

FIDELINE *(shouting loudly into the empty house)*: I hope you all die!

*(Long silence.)*

*(MARIE-HENRIETTE goes to the bay window.)*

VOICES *(outside near the house)*: Hurry! Hurry! Faster!

*(MARIE-HENRIETTE goes back to the chair and falls into a reverie, her elbows on her knees.)*

*(Long silence.)*

OTHER VOICES: There goes one, there goes another!... They're falling, they're falling! All the stars are falling into the sea!

STILL OTHER VOICES: Here, over here!...

MARIE-HENRIETTE *(shudders, gets to her feet and listens. In a whisper)*: Oh, no! No!

VOICES *(fading away)*: Come on, come on!

*(Silence.)*

MARIE-HENRIETTE *(in a sweet, supplicating, humming voice, a voice tinged with affection)*: Walter, don't call out my name any more!... Forget me for just this one night, I beg you... Can't you see the tears in my eyes? *(Softly protesting)*: No! I want to sleep, I don't want not to die... I prefer sleeping in my room tonight. There are flowers on the wallpaper there, looking at me with their tiny eyes. *(Mimicking WALTER's grave voice)*: Oh, I'd be scared of them!

VOICES: Into the shallows! The shallows!

MARIE-HENRIETTE *(smiling benignly)*: You go to sleep too... Open your window a little and in the morning you'll wake up with rosy cheeks... *(Lowering her voice)*: You want to hear a story before you go to sleep? Even though I'm quite grown up, I used to be told stories. *(Imperiously, in WALTER's voice)*: "If you want to die with me, you have to come now!" *(Brightly)*: This one. *(Declaiming in a rhythmic and monotonous voice, as though reciting a lesson)*: "The rootless trees feeding off the sky were carried aloft by their fruit. They went, inventing landscapes, from one realm to another..." Be quiet, Walter! "The rivers, so as to know everything first, kept changing course..." (those are the words I remember...) "and since their water remembered only by reflecting the grass..." Are you asleep?... "you could learn the wonders of the earth..." *(Gravely repeating WALTER's words)*: "Why don't you want to die with me?..." *(Without missing a beat, all in one breath)*: Hush now, close your eyes... *(Declaiming in gloomy despair)*: "The little princess would fly across skies as green as the grass in May. She would raise her gown to avoid catching it on the tips of the stars... (Hush, hush)... And during the night she'd go barefoot along the Milky Way, skipping from moon to moon..." *(Mimicking WALTER's voice again)*: I'm waiting for you. Are you coming or not? *(Reproachfully)*: Oh! You're not asleep yet, you bad boy! *(She bursts into tears.)*

*(Silence.)*

*(We hear an agitated music, sometimes near, sometimes far away, according to how the wind blows in and out of the house.)*

LOUD VOICES: The ship! Quick, to the pier! Wave your handkerchiefs! Farewell! The flag's been raised! Oh! It's leaving... *(The loud complaint of a siren. The VOICES grow fainter.)* There'll be a mist, the weather's so warm... and lightning...

MARIE-HENRIETTE *(imitating the high-pitched voices, phrase by phrase)*: Oh, my god! What a disaster! How will we get her out? The boathook will tear her apart! There's no more bleeding... She's so wet!... And so swollen, she looks like she's laughing. Can anyone tell who she is? Yes, yes, the little stone in her ring! She's certainly changed! "Is it my fault? That's the last straw." *(Calling out, quite loudly:)* Marie-Henriette! *(Having been carried away by her game, she suddenly awakens at the sound of her own voice. She gets up and anxiously looks around. Almost inaudibly:)* Help me! Help me!

*(Enter MADAME MERCENIER.)*

MARIE-HENRIETTE *(rushing towards her with a cry of relief)*: Mama! Mama!...

MADAME MERCENIER *(pushing her away)*: Get away from me...

MARIE-HENRIETTE *(pleadingly)*: Ma?...

MADAME MERCENIER *(forcefully)*: No, no! Go away! I don't even want to know you! When I called you before, you ignored me!... Don't pretend you didn't hear me! *(MARIE-HENRIETTE stands as if rooted to the floor while her mother passes before her, complaining in a weary voice:)* I don't have any children, I'm left all alone... What'll I do? I never thought I'd live for so long in such pain... *(She goes to the cupboard and takes out a tray with a tea set, which she'll carry to the end of the scene.)* Your father, poor man, and you, such a disobedient child, that's what I have to put up with. You're both alike; neither wicked nor good: there's no understanding between us... Is this what I was born for? Go and find Walter, why don't you?... I'll put the house on the market. *(MADAME passes in front of her daughter again who, very pale now, stares after her.)* My hair's turned white. Go on, go and don't come back; that's what I want. *(Very brief pause.)* Now!

*(She walks towards the door.)*

MARIE-HENRIETTE *(stammering)*: Mother?

MADAME MERCENIER *(sighing deeply)*: I'm shutting the doors... and that's final!

*(Exit MADAME MERCENIER.)*

*(MARIE-HENRIETTE watches her go. Her chin trembles. She doesn't move for quite a long while. Feeling abandoned by everyone, she stands there motionless. A discordant relentless music gusts in through the big bay window.)*

VOICES: Come quickly!... I'm waiting for you!

*(MARIE-HENRIETTE lowers her head, turns on her heel and goes slowly towards the street door.)*

VOICES: No, no! I'm not coming... Tomorrow... Good night...

*(Laughter outside. MARIE-HENRIETTE leans against the door, her hand on the doorknob.)*

*(Silence. Then music.)*

*(THE WOMAN appears at the door to the stairs. She looks rapidly from left to right. Seeing no one ? or has she seen MARIE-HENRIETTE?? continues talking to ZULMA on the staircase behind her.)*

THE WOMAN *(in a whisper)*: My trunks will go in the car. The porters will wait for me on the quay. You understand?

ZULMA: Yes, madame…

THE WOMAN: I don't want to wake anyone.

ZULMA *(knowingly)*: No one. I understand…

THE WOMAN: Don't knock on my door; I'll leave it open. Go. *(As ZULMA goes, she calls her back.)* It's only you who knows I'm leaving. Don't tell!

ZULMA *(blushing with pride)*: Oh! no, no!…

THE WOMAN: I know I can rely on you. Go, child. Tell the driver I'm downstairs. Thank you.

*(About to go, ZULMA comes back.)*

ZULMA *(excited, all in one breath)*: Madame!… He's coming! He's right behind you!

*(ZULMA runs past THE MAN, staring at him with amused curiosity.)*

THE WOMAN, *standing still, smiling)*: Now I'm the one waiting for you!

*(She reaches towards him. He takes her hands, caressing his face with them as a child would.)*

THE MAN: Forgive me!…

THE WOMAN *(in a burst of lighthearted laughter, mockingly)*: Oh, now that's how it is! "Forgive me." That's all he can come up with! He is already my master, this man! *(Walking backwards, she leads him to the bay window. All of a sudden she seems painfully surprised, so much so that she draws him close and puts her arms around him. Then, still laughing, but with a muffled, tender mirth, she begins to console him:)* Oh! come now, it can't be as bad as all that! Why suffer so? How many hearts do you have? I was happy when I came here. Don't try to keep me too long. I need my rest after a day like this. *(She sits down but can't keep from laughing again. With a look of coquettish mockery:)* I didn't think you were such a child!… *(He sits down on the floor, very close to her.)* You always looked so serious, so determined. And now you seem weak! So thankful for a kind word, a kind look: a reward for being a good little boy!… Men are such children! All of them! We let them have their way just so they won't cry!

THE MAN (*watching her attentively, a little tensely*): Did I cry?

THE WOMAN (*bending towards him and speaking quickly with a pretense of happiness, almost as a provocation*): And what if I left here tomorrow? Imagine: the porters come at dawn, they take everything away, and I follow! No one's awake… They leave nothing behind, nothing, not a trace. Wouldn't you cry then?

THE MAN (*after first giving a start of surprise, calmly*): You promised not to leave.

THE WOMAN (*with almost cruel intensity*): If I left tomorrow before you woke up? Without a trace, nothing, ever?

THE MAN (*smiling*): I refuse to believe it.

THE WOMAN (*laughing, very loudly*): My master speaks again! (*And as he turns away, astonished by this cruelty, she raises his head with her hand and says with melancholy tenderness:*) It's nothing… it's nothing… I'd cry too… (*In the silence that follows, as she sees MARIE-HENRIETTE.*) Marie-Henriette, what are you doing there in the shadows, child?

MARIE-HENRIETTE (*smiling wanly*): Walter's waiting for me…

THE WOMAN: Outside on the beach? (*The girl lowers her head.*) Why don't you go and meet him? Did they tell you not to? (*After a silence:*) Did you have a fight?

MARIE-HENRIETTE (*bursting out*): Oh, no, poor boy! (*She blushes.*)

THE WOMAN (*smiling*): Then go and meet him. Quickly! He shouldn't have to wait.

MARIE-HENRIETTE (*with a childish and fearful surprise*): He shouldn't? (*She sighs.*) I'll go…

VOICES OUTSIDE: Look, there must be more than twenty lights on the sea!

OTHER VOICES: The fishermen going out with the tide.

(*THE WOMAN looks briefly at MARIE-HENRIETTE. Then she turns towards THE MAN and glides close to him.*)

THE WOMAN (*low voice, rather quickly*): I want them all to be happy; you and all the others, and I myself, who may already be happy!… When I was very young, I was always a little sad. And yet I lacked for nothing,

nothing whatever. I was waiting for something that never came, something so sweet that... *(In a deeply sorrowful voice:)* I wonder what it was? *(She pulls herself together and makes herself sound happier.)* I waited for it to come, from the sun, from the trees, from the shadows of the birds, from whatever it is that makes a person happy. The finer the day, the more festive the day, the more I'd sigh. Alas, it never came! The world seemed incomplete, which made me even sadder. And ever since, my joys have been mixed with sadness... *(She stops. THE MAN looks at her tenderly. She seems lost in thought and then, in a wounded voice:)* What can I do for you before tomorrow?

THE MAN *(a little anxious, a little shy)*: I've seen you only once without your veil.

*(Suddenly she raises her veil. Even in the softening lamp light, her face startles him by its brightness, its astonishing unnatural brightness.)*

*(Leaning over him, she waits, reckless of the danger.)*

THE WOMAN *(slowly)*: Look: do you see me well enough now? Is that better? Look: I'm covered with makeup, painted... *(After a moment's hesitation, in conflict with herself, in a low voice:)* ... Already old. *(A pause.)* You can't believe it? *(He looks at her, dumbfounded. She sits, letting her veil fall back, and laughs.)* He won't believe it! *(Without a pause, strangely overcome:)* Oh, my God! I'm tired!...

THE MAN *(imploringly)*: Your hands, Elisabeth! I haven't seen your hands!

THE WOMAN *(quickly, very upset)*: No, no, no, not yet! *(Joyously, hiding her nervousness:)* I need to make them beautiful first, to polish my nails, to put on my rings! *(Abruptly, for no apparent reason, with delirious pride:)* Once a pauper bought me flowers on the street and offered them to me!... Once I swam naked in the sea! *(Crushed again by enormous fatigue, but making a piteous effort to rid herself of her torment:)* I don't have the strength to shame myself before you. Though that's what I should do—for then I would be free...

THE MAN *(smiling, with tenderness)*: I didn't ask for your secret. Bear the weight of your life by yourself. This is the last night.

THE WOMAN: You don't understand me, I always lie... *(Sighing, she turns to MARIE-HENRIETTE standing silently by the door.)* Well, child, aren't you going? *(Instead, feeling vulnerable, MARIE-HENRIETTE slips close to her like a little hunted animal. Lovingly, THE WOMAN draws her close. The music *outside builds, its rhythm, that of a joyless dance.)* Walter's waiting for you, growing cold with impatience. He feels lost without you… *(MARIE-HENRI-ETTE drops her head.)* Sleepy? More than anything else you feel sad, don't you, Marie-Henriette?

MARIE-HENRIETTE: Oh, yes!...

THE WOMAN *(moved)*: Poor child, why is that?...

MARIE-HENRIETTE *(trying not to cry)*: I don't know…

THE WOMAN: Go and find your little friend. He'll make you feel better. *(MARIE-HENRIETTE says nothing.)* You'd rather stay with us?

MARIE-HENRIETTE: I don't know…

THE WOMAN: Well, then stay! *(She turns back to THE MAN. Mockingly:)* Young as she is, she knows all the wiles of weakness. She's just like me! *(Then with remarkable energy:)* I wanted to take revenge on you for your sweetness. It was such a burden to me. After I left you on the beach, I saw that a man was following me, stopping whenever I stopped, not daring to come close, stalking me like a wolf; and so I smiled to encourage him.

THE MAN *(growing pale)*: Elisabeth!

THE WOMAN *(with a challenging laugh)*: I hardly heard what he said to me. Oh, how he loved me, that one. He'd have offered me money, I think. I took the arm he held out…

THE MAN *(grabbing her wrist and twisting it hard)*: Be quiet!

THE WOMAN *(with a cry of great pain and revulsion)*: You brute!

THE MAN *(fiercely angry)*: You're a fool!...

*(They stand facing each other like enemies, petrified by this violent turn of events.)*

*(Long silence.)*

THE WOMAN *(looking at him with profound surprise)*: Who are you?

THE MAN *(numbly, tormented)*: Why do you hurt those who love you?

THE WOMAN *(with a bitter laugh)*: They're the only ones I can touch! *(Pulling MARIE-HENRIETTE close to her again and holding her tight. In a positive transport of love for her:)* Dearest child, dearest child! Don't be frightened… Be wiser than we are, show more compassion. Go to Walter now.

MARIE-HENRIETTE *(frightened, clinging to her)*: Oh! No, no, no!

THE WOMAN *(sweetly, persuasively)*: Yes, now you're afraid; but once outside, you'll be happy! Come with me, come. I'll take you by the hand and walk you to the door. Come… *(Pulling her.)* Where is he waiting?

MARIE-HENRIETTE *(in a dull voice)*: On the beach, where the water is shallow…

THE WOMAN *(enveloping her in her shawl)*: He's been waiting for so long! He's been calling for you oh so softly. But someone's heard him and now he's ashamed!… Go…

*(She opens the door to the beach.)*

MARIE-HENRIETTE *(stopping, speaking quickly with shallow breaths)*: What if I don't go? Maybe then he'll come back, and tomorrow the sun will be shining and he won't be unhappy! He'll love me…

THE WOMAN: No, not another word… Go now, I want you to go! Quickly!

*(She pushes MARIE-HENRIETTE towards the door.)*

Adieu…

MARIE-HENRIETTE *(with a piteous smile, breathlessly)*: How funny the room looks… Farewell.

*(She goes out, still looking back at the room.)*

THE WOMAN *(at the doorstep)*: We'll wait for you here, near the lamp. *(Half closing the door:)* Quickly, quickly!…

*(She shuts the door.)*

THE MAN *(leaning out the bay window)*: Run now, run, Marie-Henriette! The breeze is so light, the flags hardly stir. The stars are out and there's a new moon. *(THE WOMAN joins him at the window. He smiles at her.)* Now she hesitates!

ELISABETH *(shouting in a light, joyful voice)*: Run, child, run! Tuck up your skirt, dance barefoot in the foam!… Good night!…

*(Short pause.)*

THE MAN *(happily)*: She's gone!… *(He sits by the bay window. ELISABETH stays by his side, gazing out at the sea. He speaks softly, in the great silent void of the night:)* The moonlight's slowly dimming all the lights on the pier. Look how sea and sky reflect each other as in a magic mirror. I'm so far from you, Elisabeth! So near you, too! *(Accompanied by the clear sounds of laughter outside:)* The pilings' black shapes in the shimmering. They're like signposts to who knows where. The gulls are asleep on the opposite cliff... Primeval man must have seen this same light on these shores. What hourglass could count the age of the ocean, not even one filled with all of the sand on all of the world's beaches? Let's sail forever to the horizon in that little boat, with its green light blinking... No, there, at the end of the pier! *(He takes ELISABETH's hand.)* I see your tears... Forget my anger, Elisabeth. I didn't realize how much you needed to protect yourself against. It's the last night! *(After a short pause:)* To leave! Yet out there with the fishermen, we'd turn our faces back to shore; and the unknown fear which drives us would be behind the lighted windows, the windows of others... And why? Only the great Sphinx of Gizah knows the loneliness of the desert where caravans are lost... Elisabeth, your little hand is trembling; are you cold?... *(She shakes her head. He stands up.)* Here men are carried away by winds, by tides, by stars, away! away! their little heads under the infinite sky! *(In the distance the music fades into heartrending regrets and suddenly sounds trite. He pulls ELISABETH close to him, but she utters a frightened cry and pulls away from the window.)* What's the matter?

ELISABETH *(in a dull voice)*: Somebody's out there, spying on us!

THE MAN *(quickly)*: Where?

ELISABETH: There, in front of the window! *(THE MAN leans out. She regains her composure.)* I was frightened...

THE MAN *(lightly)*: Was it that old man who's always prowling about?

ELISABETH *(heavily)*: Yes, I recognized his shadow. *(With energy:)* What does he want from me? I don't know him!...

THE MAN: He used to live here, before we arrived.

ELISABETH *(with a sigh)*: Maybe so... *(She tries to look less upset. In vain.)* Is he still there?

THE MAN: Calm yourself, he's moving away... Fideline torments him, they say (how exactly, I don't know), and every day he begs her...

ELISABETH *(obsessively)*: I don't even know his name, I know nothing about him, nothing!

THE MAN: He's a sick old man, crushed, hunched over, hideous!

*(ELISABETH bursts out with a dry, mocking laugh, which appears to stupefy THE MAN.)*

ELISABETH: Sick, old, crushed, hunched over, hideous! Oh! oh! finished! Hopeless and childless! Too old, too old, too old!

THE MAN *(troubled, not understanding)*: Elisabeth?

ELISABETH *(with a gaiety that's almost sincere)*: And for now, good night!... Let's go to our rooms. I need sleep, and you're restless. Good night...

MADAME MERCENIER *(offstage, in a loud, anxious voice)*: Marie-Henriette! Marie-Henriette! *(Alarmed by her voice, ELISABETH and THE MAN almost relax their embrace and they stand there, wordless, apprehensive.)* Marie-Henriette! Riette!... *(She enters with a tray full of cups. She puts the tray down. Not seeing her daughter, she almost faints.)* She isn't here?... Where is she?

THE MAN: She just left.

MADAME MERCENIER *(in a panic)*: She's gone! *(Groans:)* Oh lord! I knew it! *(Calling towards the kitchen:)* Zulma, come quickly, Zulma!... *(Collapsing on a chair.)* Where is she? I remember now, when I was crossing the room, she looked more lonely than usual... Zulma!...

THE WOMAN *(surprised)*: She went to meet Walter of course.

MADAME MERCENIER *(angrily)*: Who cares who she went to meet! *(In a softer voice, drawing out her words:)* I remember now, I remember!

*(Enter ZULMA smiling.)*

*MADAME MERCENIER (standing up)*: My daughter's gone. She probably went to Walter's house, or else she's on the beach... Go out and look for her, look everywhere, girl! Shout her name! *(She sits down again. Stammering:)* She looked as pale and cold as a stone... Riette, Riette!... She needed me same as when she was sick. Surely she did! *(To ZULMA, enraged:)* Haven't you gone yet?

ZULMA *(with a shrug of her shoulders)*: There's plenty of time to look for her!

MADAME MERCENIER *(desperate for hope)*: Yes, yes, you're right. Oh god, what's happening to me? I haven't suffered like this since the day she was born. *(Biting her lip, she sits down and puts her hands in her lap.)* Go on, go on, you stupid child, and don't come back alone! *(She stands.)* Tell her I'm exhausted and I want to say good night to her before I lie down... I want to kiss her... Don't forget anything. I'm shaking like it's winter, but I'm not crying!

*(Exit MADAME MERCENIER.)*

ZULMA *(giggling)*: She's hiding in the shadows with Walter!

THE MAN: You'll find them down on the dunes or at the old harbor on the pier. That's where he was waiting for her.

ZULMA: Amen!

*(Exit ZULMA.)*

ELISABETH *(amused as she watches ZULMA walk away)*: What a wild creature she is! She leaps and bounds like a young animal!

THE MAN *(kissing the back of ELISABETH's neck)*: Your hair smells like bark and resin... Let down your hair, Elisabeth!

ELISABETH *(laughing girlishly)*: Please stop that. I'm at the end of my strength... *(Suddenly, with terror and despair:)* He's back! There, can't you see him!

THE MAN: The old man?

ELISABETH *(numbly)*: Yes... the old man... You'd say someone was out there watching him from the shadows: a woman...

THE MAN *(at the window)*: He lived here so long, he must be home-sick? *(He goes to ELISABETH.)* So what?

ELISABETH *(discouraged)*: You're right, so what, so what... *(Smiling wearily.)* Oh, my dear, won't you please let me go? I can't stay awake any longer without the most childish fears. This lovely night's haunted by demons for me! Truly, I'm overwhelmed... Please let me go!

THE MAN *(holding her)*: I want to sing you a lullaby, to cradle you in my arms and rock you to sleep... Good night.

ELISABETH *(tenderly, warding him off with her hand)*: No, no more kisses! Good night.

THE MAN *(still holding her close as she tries to get free)*: Tomorrow you'll offer me your bare arms, your bare hands!...

ELISABETH *(begging him)*: Oh, please say good night...

THE MAN: …and your little bare feet whose prints the sea molds with mother-of-pearl, when you go to sleep with the mermaids!

ELISABETH *(with an angry laugh)*: Stop all this nonsense, I beg you!… You're out of your mind. *(She struggles to get free.)* I love you too… but you wouldn't treat a defenseless child the way you're treating me. *(She throws her arms around him and forces him down in the chair next to the bay window.)* Enough, sit down in the chair, put this pillow behind your head and stay there… Yes, stay!… Let go of me now. They can see us.

THE MAN *(mockingly)*: The old man?

ELISABETH *(numbly)*: Him too. *(Pauses.)* Stay still, be quiet, close your eyes… *(Leaning over him.)* Quietly now, let me leave… *(She kisses him.)* There… We'd go on saying goodbye till morning if it were up to you! I'm kissing you for the last time. Pretend you're asleep and I'll go quietly…

THE MAN *(closing his eyes and lying back)*: Good night…

ELISABETH *(slowly walking backwards towards the door to the stairs and speaking with a despairing softness)*: You won't see me go… Be still! If you love me, you won't open your eyes… I don't want to know what I'm losing by leaving… How long the hours will be without you!… *(Leaning against the door frame, she bends her head down and starts to weep but immediately regains control of herself and says distinctly:)* Sleep, sleep soundly! I'll never forget this day, not one shadow, not one reflection, not one sigh…

THE MAN *(in a low voice)*: Your voice is an oasis in the burning silence.

ELISABETH *(tenderly reprimanding)*: Oh, you're not asleep yet, you naughty boy!

*(Suddenly the street door opens and an exuberant ZULMA bursts in. THE MAN stands up and confronts her.)*

ZULMA: Yes! Yes! It's me! I couldn't get to the lighthouse before those three devils started chasing me! The cutest rascals in town… I wouldn't have known which to choose. Come into the moonlight with us! I said to myself, Zulma, quick, get into the house or else two of you will come home without Marie-Henriette! *(With a sigh of relief:)* Thank you very much!

*(ELISABETH has slipped into the shadow of the stairs where she is invisible.)*

THE MAN *(surprised, calls out)*: Elisabeth!

*(Long pause.)*

ZULMA (*smiling*): She's slipped away like a shadow! (*Looking outdoors and bursting out laughing, her hands on her hips.*) Aha! There he is: the most faithful of my beaux followed me to the corner! (*Mockingly:*) Boo!... Boo!...

THE MAN: Marie-Henriette's still missing. Her poor mother.

ZULMA: What do you mean, her poor mother? She goes out every night. When I call, she pretends not to hear. If I go out again, my three boyfriends will be all over me! (*She turns back to the door and then cries out in a panic:*) Madame! What's that? Madame! It's Baron Cazou.

(*She backs away, frightened. THE MAN watches with intense curiosity.*)

THE MAN (*in a low voice*): Cazou?...

(*CAZOU enters but only halfway.*)

CAZOU (*imploringly*): Zulma, my child, don't shout. Fideline wanted this... She'll beat me! Yes, yes... She's here, Fideline, right in front of the door.

ZULMA (*calling again*): Madame! Madame!

FIDELINE (*outside*): Zulma!

CAZOU (*coming into the room*): It's nothing...

ZULMA (*at the door*): Is that you, Fideline? What did you say? He's wants to come in? Yes, yes, I'm coming!... (*She turns towards THE MAN.*) Maybe she'll go with me, I'm off...

(*Exit ZULMA.*)

(*CAZOU and THE MAN are alone.*)

CAZOU (*with a timid little smile*): It's nothing whatever. M'sieur Cazou, Baron Cazou, that's right... (*Leaning over his shadow and snapping his fingers:*) Down, Sultan, down! Down, black dog!... (*Explaining:*) That's my shadow. He's all I have. (*As before:*) Down! Down! (*Weeping like a child:*) No one else loves him. (*Begging shamelessly:*) For pity's sake, spare a lump of sugar for a poor, starving animal? Won't you, please?... (*He backs toward the table where the lamp is. Then raising his arms and playing with his shadow, he turns round and round.*) Hop! Hop! Up!... That's a good boy... Now down! Where's your master?... Look!

THE MAN (*still in a low voice*): Cazou?

CAZOU (*with childish satisfaction*): He's a happy dog! Yes, isn't he a happy

*79*

dog? But he's losing his hair… *(Grimacing, he fusses with his clothes. Suddenly, suppressing his sobs:)* None of it's real, it's all just for laughs, a comedy… *(Shaking his head, he looks down at the ground in misery.)*

THE MAN *(incredulously)*: Are you really Cazou? Baron Cazou?…

CAZOU *(with great dignity)*: Oh yes, I am. Indeed I am. Jean… Louis… Frédéric… It's all written down!

THE MAN *(moved)*: I remember… *(Taking his arm and leading him to the chair:)* Come over here and sit down, old man. You must be tired.

CAZOU *(sighing)*: Oh, yes, yes, terribly tired!… Tonight Fideline will sing me to sleep. A lullaby… She *has* to! *(Adding mysteriously:)* She's waiting for me out on the street… "Hush," she said, "hush! Go into the house and tell him…" Tell him what? I've already forgotten. *(He moans.)*

THE MAN *(with compassion)*: Don't torment yourself. There now, are you feeling better? Do you need anything?

CAZOU *(humbly)*: A little sugar, yes, for the good beast… *(As he says this, he reaches for the sugar bowl, hand shaking with greed. Then, very rapidly:)* Thank you, thank you! Oh, thank you!… *(Laughing a lively little laugh.)* You'll protect me this evening, won't you, Sultan? *(Reprovingly:)* Quiet now, good dog! *(Gluttonously, he starts sucking on his sugar cube.)*

THE MAN *(softly, in a dreamy voice)*: I remember!… *(Leaning over CAZOU.)* How well I know you! You'll never guess! Cazou and the Princess! I was seven, maybe eight, years old, and I heard about you every night. My father took me all over Europe… He had ancestors everywhere. He was looking for a place to call home. And wherever we went, Cazou and the Princess had been there before! I remember! I remember!… I was shown your footprints on the snowy slopes of mountains, on the burning sands of beaches. "The Princess and Cazou!" And, once, your initials carved in the bark of a tree in an almost forgotten forest. It seemed that in every shadow on earth, there was the shadow of your love!… Later, I actually saw you! *(Somewhat impassioned, with fond emotion:)* You and she were walking together, immersed in sunlight on the banks of a dazzling river, I don't remember where. People run after you waving their hands and calling your names. "What have they done?" I asked Father. "They are beautiful," he replied. You were straight and tall, with so gallant an air, modest and a little aloof. And the docile Princess, at your side, gazing at you with a joyous smile. I couldn't get it out of my head. "But what have they done, what have they done?" I insisted on knowing why you deserved such acclaim! "They are beautiful," my father said, "and they love each other more than anything in the world!" *(Brief pause.)* Odd how it's all coming back to me now!... I saw you a few years later, in Paris. You were alone. Your hair was going grey at the temples. I followed you for a very long time on that terrace where you were watching blindly, wrapped in wet fog. *(Dreaming now.)* People still admired you, but nobody shouted your name anymore. You came there every day. Don't you remember?

CAZOU *(surprised, childishly)*: No, no, he doesn't know anymore...

THE MAN: Try to remember. It was the year of the regicides... You were wearing a ring with a big black stone. Remember?

CAZOU: Nothing...nothing...

THE MAN *(laughing softly)*: As for me, I always had a picture of the Princess beside my bed (I wonder where I lost it?). I was so much in love with her, you'd have been jealous if you'd known! I avoided you! *(Eyes half closed, with a sudden tenderness:)* Princess Groulingen... *(He says this in almost a whisper and yet...)*

CAZOU *(in the ensuing silence)*: Elisabeth.

THE MAN *(stupefied)*: What are you saying?

CAZOU *(with a vain gravity)*: Elisabeth, yes, yes, yes, yes... *(THE MAN stands up, disturbed, and stares a long time at CAZOU, who seems to be stroking his shadow and murmuring:)* Quiet, Sultan, quiet, boy!... Oh, you little black devil!...

THE MAN *(after a long silence, strangely)*: Elisabeth? Yes, Elisabeth von Groulingen... *(Recovering, very joyfully:)* I hid from you, like a hare in the bushes... I loved her with a purity which absolved me forever of sin! Elisabeth?... I was scared of being discovered. *(Sitting back down, inquisitively:)* Why did she leave you?

CAZOU *(in agony)*: Why?... She left...

THE MAN: How did it happen? Try to remember.

CAZOU *(stupidly)*: ... She left... *(He groans:)* I can't, my head's empty... It's over...

THE MAN: No doubt she died?

CAZOU *(surprised)*: She died? *(And then he laughs his lively, childish laugh.)* Oh, no, no, no, no. That woman was immortal!...

THE MAN: Where is she now? Where is she?

*(CAZOU stands up, timidly overcome with joy.)*

CAZOU *(chuckling)*: She's here! Yes, that's what Fideline said. She said, "She's here! That's what you'll tell them." Now her words come back to me... Ha! Ha! "She's here!"

THE MAN *(stupefied, standing up)*: Here in town?

CAZOU *(very animated, with a grotesque expression of deliverance)*: Yes, in this town! Exactly, Cazou saw her, Fideline too, so did everyone else! "You'll tell the man that, like a good little boy." *(He laughs.)* She's right here in the house. Ha! Ha!

THE MAN *(uneasy)*: You're out of your mind!

CAZOU: "In the house" (those were her words!) "with the man..." That's all!

THE MAN *(brutally)*: No, no!

CAZOU *(with imbecilic obstinacy)*: Yes, yes, here!... Fideline insisted on it... "Upstairs in her room." *(To his shadow, already distracted:)* Right, Sultan, right, lazy dog?

THE MAN: Can it be?

CAZOU *(frightened)*: She's here... Say it, please, or I'll get a beating... The wicked girl insisted! She's here, have pity on me...

THE MAN *(tensely)*: You're lying!

CAZOU *(sobbing piteously)*: Poor Cazou... She'll take all his money and leave him... Say yes, my friend, say yes, won't you please? She'll burn my cane...

THE MAN *(laughing but still concerned)*: Ha! The old fool! His nightmare is contagious! *(With sudden fury:)* Shut up! Shut up! You're lying!

CAZOU *(sniveling)*: Have pity...

THE MAN *(revolted, disgusted)*: Oh, spare me your faces! Go away!

CAZOU *(backing away, in a timid voice)*: Oh, don't shout at him anymore.

THE MAN *(fighting against the obvious)*: Elisabeth! *(To CAZOU:)* Go away! *(Shrugging, he says mockingly:)* Ah! She too was afraid... No, you're making me laugh! "Childless. I'm alone. Too old, too old!" *(Stricken:)* What?

*(With fury:)* You're lying! She didn't even know your name! Get out. *(Laughing again.)* Grotesque old ghost haunting the living with your clumping footsteps! Pathetic obsession!... *(Calling out imperiously:)* Elisabeth! Elisabeth! What? She doesn't hide her hands, she didn't want to put on her rings! Elisabeth! *(He goes to CAZOU, grabs him by his lapels and shakes him:)* Get out!... Why are you still living, ghastly child! Get out!...

CAZOU *(terrified)*: Help! Help!

THE MAN *(suddenly compassionate)*: Ah, no, it was all a bad dream... *(He puts his hands on CAZOU's shoulders and says with sad cordiality:)* Go now, don't be afraid. Poor lost soul, go and rest in peace... *(Then overcome with disgust, he spits in the old man's face.)* Stinking corpse! *(He rushes to the stairs and yells out in anger:)* Elisabeth! Elisabeth!

CAZOU *(alone, joyfully wiping the spit off his face with his coat sleeve)*: It didn't hurt a bit, not a bit... *(Then he calls weakly out the front door:)* Fideline!... Fideline!...

FIDELINE *(appearing in the doorway)*: And now, come quickly! Give me your hand! *(With sugary irony:)* He'll get a treat, the cutie pie! *(Laughing wickedly.)* Faster. Gather up your belongings, Harlequin!

*(They leave. A silence.)*

VOICE OF THE MAN *(from upstairs, loud, hurried, anxious)*: Elisabeth! Open the door! The door, Elisabeth! I insist!

*(Another silence, then the sound of breaking glass.)*

VOICE OF ELISABETH *(fierce, distraught)*: Never again! Never again! *(Her heartrending voice comes closer, filling the space with her terrified cries.)* No more light! Blind yourself! *(And ELISABETH in full flight leaps into the room, which she traverses like a shadow, exclaiming:)* Farewell! Poke out your eyes! No more light! Blind yourself!

*(She reaches the other side of the room.)*

THE MAN *(calling out in a biting voice)*: Elisabeth von Groulingen!

*(She turns at the very moment when THE MAN turns on the chandelier and a blinding light fills the room. THE WOMAN stands before him without her makeup. She is still a beautiful woman, but her beauty is faded and distant. Very pale, with discolored lips and heavy lids, her gray hair in disarray, she clutches the folds of her nightdress to her desiccated breast. With no mystery left, she is now a figure both tragic and grotesque.*

*THE MAN utters a cry of surprise, mixed with profound sorrow.*

*Very long silence.)*

THE WOMAN (*stammering, lamenting*): Tomorrow I'll be gone… I'm also being punished… I'm not what I was… Soon I'll be gone…

*(THE MAN laughs, not a violent, bitter and sarcastic laugh, but one of peculiar disappointment at not being able to help. He walks slowly towards the door, tilting a little away from her, with his hands held up in front of his face, making futile little gestures of protest and tenderness.)*

THE MAN: I'm not laughing… I'm not laughing… Elisabeth… I'm not laughing!…

*(THE MAN exits in this manner. THE WOMAN gasps, never taking her eyes off of him.)*

*(Finally she falls softly to the floor, her face in her hands and her knees pulled up. She seems to be no more than a pile of rags in a corner of the room.)*

*(Someone peeks into the room from the street and inspects the room.)*

A VOICE: She isn't there… Go on in.

*(Enter ZULMA in tears, her face buried in her apron, supported, helped, surrounded by a silent crowd of neighbors.)*

WOMEN (*speaking in low voices, very fast*): She'll understand if you're crying!… Don't be afraid! After all, it isn't your child!…

ZULMA (*sobbing*): How can I do it?

WOMEN (*rapidly, drowning each other out*): I was the first one there… No, *I* was first! I was on the other side of the harbor… Such beautiful children. Oh, the torment of being a mother! We all heard a loud noise: "*splash*" and that was it, yes, that was it…

ZULMA (*raising her tear-stained face*): Why do I have to be the one to tell her? Why me? I'm the stupid one, I don't dare!…

WOMEN: Lelubre pulled them out with his hook. They were heavy. Yes, but he's strong!

ZULMA (*with all the uncertainty of her despair*): And not even a note for her poor mother, not a word! The ingratitude!

WOMEN (*faster and faster*): Who's going to tell Walter's parents? His mother's always away somewhere... I've got a daughter too, a serious girl, I hope she's fast asleep in her bed... They were tied together around the waist! They fought each other before they died, scratching, biting. They already hated each other... Don't tell the mother that!... Oh, no!...

ZULMA (*sobbing*): Shut up! Shut up!

WOMEN: I think she called out "mother" before she drowned. Tell her that, Zulma. And then she cried out "My God!" Too late! Better stick with "mother," she'll like that...

(*Enter MADAME MERCENIER.*

*All the women turn towards her, their faces fixed in expressions of dread. Immediately she understands. Petrified, she stops a little way off from them. Then she starts rocking back and forth, her fist pressed to her mouth. She utters a sort of sweet keening sound, continuous and poignant.*)

MADAME MERCENIER (*calling out at last in a crushed, full-throated voice*): Marie-Henriette!... Marie-Henriette!... It's true?... You've left me forever? Marie-Henriette! Maya, you tell me? My beautiful naughty daughter!... (*Begging of the neighbors, abasing herself:*) She's still mine, I want to see her... Tell me, Yette, Yette. I promise not to make a scene, scratching my face with my nails... I won't scream too loud, I promise... Tell me, Maya, tell me? I bit my lip, but it doesn't hurt much... Tell, Marie-Henriette, tell? (*She walks towards the door. As she approaches, the neighbors fall back. She goes into the crowd, enveloped by two rows of silent spectators.*) My treasure! Only an hour ago she could laugh and run and play and open and close her eyes!

(*She exits. Behind her, as in the wake of a heavy ship, the waves of neighbors close up and follow her.*)

A WOMAN (*supporting ZULMA, the last to leave*): You saw how she almost swallowed her handkerchief and then pulled it back out slowly, inch by inch, between her clenched teeth!

(*Enter QUASIMENT, arms raised, already outraged.*)

QUASIMENT: Nobody here? They've all left, the magpies! (*About to close the door to the street, shouting:*) You think I didn't hear you? All the same, I knew you were here from the way the wind moved the curtains!... What'd you say?


CURTAIN


*85*

This translation of *Mad for Love*
was printed in Garamond.

Also available

Fernand Crommelynck
*The Magnificent Cuckold*
(*Le Cocu magnifique*)
Translated by Ben Sonnenberg *&* Amiel Melnick